# NO FRILLS Exam Prep Books

## Intellectual Properties, Trademarks and Copyrights

ExamREVIEW.NET (a.k.a. ExamREVIEW) is an independent content developer not associated/affiliated with the certification vendor(s) mentioned throughout this book. The name(s), title(s) and award(s) of the certification exam(s) mentioned in this book are the trademark(s) of the respective certification vendor(s). We mention these name(s) and/or the relevant terminologies only for describing the relevant exam process(es) and knowledge.

> We are NOT affiliated with Microsoft. This book is also NOT endorsed by Microsoft. The MTA exams are the property of Microsoft. Windows Server is the trademark of Microsoft.

ExamREVIEW(TM) and ExamFOCUS(TM) are our own trademarks for publishing and marketing self-developed examprep books worldwide. The EXAMREVIEW.NET web site has been created on the Internet since January 2001. The EXAMFOCUS.NET division has its web presence established since 2009.

> Copyright 2015. ExamREVIEW.NET. All rights reserved.

**Contents of this book are fully copyrighted.** We develop study material entirely on our own. Braindump is strictly prohibited. We provide essential knowledge contents, NOT any generalized "study system" kind of "pick-the-right-answer-every time" techniques or "visit this link" referrals.

## Contents Update

All books come with LIFE TIME FREE UPDATES. When you find a newer version of the purchased book all you need to do is to go and download. **Please check our web site's Free Updates section regularly:**

http://www.examreview.net/free_updates.htm

## Page Formatting and Typeface

To accommodate the needs of those with weaker vision, we use LARGER PRINT throughout the book whenever practical. The text in this book was created using Garamond (size 16). A little bit of page resizing, however, may have happened along the actual book printing process.

## The Exam

The Microsoft Technology Associate MTA certification is an entry-level certification which serves as a good starting point for students and educators who may eventually progress to the Microsoft Technology Specialist MCTS or higher programs. Simply put, it assesses the foundational knowledge necessary to pursue MCTS, MCITP or MCPD certifications. The certification focuses more on knowledge and a little less on skills. However, the knowledge areas are all based on MS products so you must know those products inside and out. Questions on the general knowledge are relatively easy. Product and technology specific technical questions, however, are way more difficult. This is why we developed this study product - we focus on those difficult topics that involve difficult technical skills. We want you to be able to answer these difficult questions and secure exam success accordingly.

Exam 98-365: Windows Server Administration Fundamentals is all about Windows Server 2008 R2. Topics covered include:

- Understanding Server Installation
- Understanding Server Roles
- Understanding Active Directory
- Understanding Storage
- Understanding Server Performance Management
- Understanding Server Maintenance

This ExamFOCUS book focuses on the more difficult topics that will likely make a difference in exam results. The book is NOT intended to guide you through every single official topic. **You should therefore use this book together with other reference books for the best possible preparation outcome. You should download the evaluation copy of Windows Server 2008 R2 and play with it. You can use it for free for max 240 days. You should download the ISO image file and burn a DVD disc out of it, then perform installation accordingly.**

Although there is a VHD version available, we do not recommend that you use it for testing. There are some complicated steps involved which may not always go as smooth.

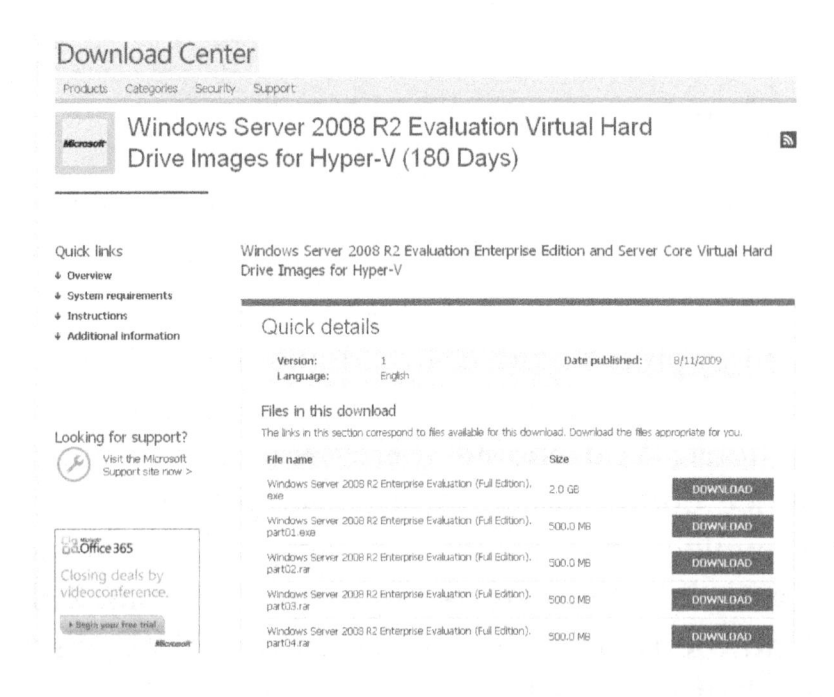

# Table of Contents (MTA Exam – WinServ 2008R2)

<u>INTELLECTUAL PROPERTIES, TRADEMARKS AND COPYRIGHTS</u> ........................ 1

<u>CONTENTS UPDATE</u> ................................................................................................ 2

<u>PAGE FORMATTING AND TYPEFACE</u> ................................................................ 2

<u>THE EXAM</u> ................................................................................................................ 2

<u>OVERVIEW OF SERVER & NETWORK PLANNING, TUNING AND MAINTENANCE</u> ........................................................................................................ 8

OVERVIEW ................................................................................................................... 8
SERVER ROLES ............................................................................................................ 9
WINDOWS SERVER OPERATING SYSTEMS OVERVIEW ......................................... 10
FILE SYSTEM AND PARTITIONS ............................................................................... 14
SMP AND MULTI-CORE PROCESSORS ..................................................................... 17
PROCESSORS AND LICENSING ................................................................................. 18
64 BIT COMPUTING AND MEMORY SUPPORT ........................................................ 19
VIRTUALIZATION, HYPER-V AND LICENSING ....................................................... 20
CLOUD COMPUTING ................................................................................................. 22
HARDWARE CAPACITY PLANNING ......................................................................... 22
STORAGE CAPACITY PLANNING ............................................................................. 23
LOAD BALANCING .................................................................................................... 26
SERVER PERFORMANCE MONITORING, MAINTENANCE AND TUNING ............. 27
SERVER TROUBLESHOOTING .................................................................................. 30
SPECIAL CONSIDERATIONS ..................................................................................... 32
NETWORK INFRASTRUCTURE AND BASIC WINDOWS NETWORKING ............... 32
OPEN SYSTEM INTERCONNECT .............................................................................. 34
ROUTING AND SWITCHING ..................................................................................... 35
IP ADDRESSING ........................................................................................................ 36
IP SUBNETTING ........................................................................................................ 39
DNS ............................................................................................................................ 40
WIRELESS BASED LOCAL AREA NETWORKING .................................................... 42
WAN NETWORKING ................................................................................................. 44
SECURITY PLANNING .............................................................................................. 45
DISASTER RECOVERY PLANS FOR SERVERS ........................................................ 47
SERVICE PACKS AND PATCHES ............................................................................... 49

## OVERVIEW OF ADMINISTRATIVE TOOLS AND OTHER INTERFACES ................ 53

SERVER MANAGEMENT UI .................................................................................. 53
MANAGING SERVICES ........................................................................................ 54
GROUP POLICY AND LOCAL POLICY ................................................................... 58
SOFTWARE RESTRICTIONS ................................................................................. 61
APPLOCKER ...................................................................................................... 63
RUNNING A PROGRAM AS AN ADMINISTRATOR ................................................... 66
INTERNET EXPLORER 8 ...................................................................................... 66
DEVICE MANAGER AND DEVICE INSTALLATION SETTINGS ................................. 69
CONFIGURING VHD ........................................................................................... 71
PARENT AND CHILD VHD .................................................................................. 73
COMMAND LINE MANAGEMENT UTILITIES ........................................................ 74

## SERVER 2008 R2 INSTALLATION AND CONFIGURATION ............................... 78

PRE-INSTALLATION PREP WORKS ....................................................................... 78
ADMINISTRATOR ACCOUNT ............................................................................... 79
MANUAL INSTALLATION VS UNATTENDED INSTALLATION .................................. 81
DISK PARTITIONING ........................................................................................... 84
DISM ................................................................................................................ 86
WINDOWS PE AND WDS ................................................................................... 88
INITIAL CONFIGURATION ................................................................................... 89
THE SERVER MIGRATION TOOL .......................................................................... 90

## NETWORK SETTINGS, SECURITY AND REMOTE/MOBILE ACCESS ............. 94

NETWORK LOCATION ........................................................................................ 94
IP V4 AND V6 .................................................................................................... 95
NETWORK SHARING AND DISCOVERY ................................................................ 96
FILE AND PRINT SERVICES ................................................................................. 98
NAME RESOLUTION ......................................................................................... 100
COMMAND LINE NETWORKING TOOLS .............................................................. 101
WINDOWS FIREWALL AND IP SECURITY POLICY .............................................. 103
IPSEC AND SSL ............................................................................................... 108
DISK BASED ENCRYPTION ................................................................................ 108
FIREWALL SECURITY ....................................................................................... 109
VIRUS SECURITY ............................................................................................. 110
WEB SERVER SECURITY .................................................................................. 110
NAME RESOLUTION SECURITY ......................................................................... 111

REMOTE MANAGEMENT ........................................................................................ 111
FOLDER REDIRECTION AND OFFLINE ACCESS ................................................. 114
DIRECTACCESS, REMOTE ACCESS AND ROUTING ............................................ 116
BRANCHCACHE ................................................................................................. 121
BITLOCKER ........................................................................................................ 122

## SYSTEM MONITORING, PERFORMANCE MANAGEMENT AND MAINTENANCE ........................................................................................................................ 128

EVENT VIEWER .................................................................................................. 128
PERFMON ........................................................................................................... 133
RESOURCE MONITORING ................................................................................... 136
POWER OPTIONS ................................................................................................ 137
VOLUME SHADOW COPY SERVICE .................................................................... 138

## USER MANAGEMENT AND BACKUP & RECOVERY ............................. 142

SHARED FOLDERS .............................................................................................. 142
USERS AND GROUPS .......................................................................................... 142
BACKUP .............................................................................................................. 146
RECOVERY OPTIONS .......................................................................................... 149
SAFE MODE AND LAST KNOWN GOOD CONFIGURATION ............................... 152

## SETTING UP ACTIVE DIRECTORY ............................................................. 155

BASIC CONCEPTS OF AD ................................................................................... 155
INSTALLING A DOMAIN CONTROLLER AND CHANGING THE FUNCTIONAL LEVEL ................. 155
ROLES AND OPERATION MASTERS ................................................................... 165
CREATING NEW FOREST, NEW CHILD DOMAIN OR NEW DOMAIN TREE .............................. 167
CREATING NEW RESOURCES, OUS AND SITES .................................................. 168
TRUSTS ............................................................................................................... 170

# Overview of Server & Network Planning, Tuning and Maintenance

## Overview

A computer network is a system for communication between individual computers. These networks may be fixed via cabling or temporary via modems or other remote connection methods. A server is a computer on a network that manages network resources. A file server is a computer and storage device dedicated to storing files. A print server is a computer that manages one or more printers. A network server is a computer that manages network traffic. A database server is a computer system that processes database queries.

**Servers are mostly dedicated, that they would perform no other tasks besides their assigned server tasks. You do not do your work on the server. You do your work on your own desktop PC, then save your works on the server.** The basic components of a server and a regular PC are the same. The two primarily differ in these aspects:

| | |
|---|---|
| • Intended use | • Number of processors |
| • Workload | • Amount of RAM |
| • Physical storage | • Specialized storage |
| | • Maintenance |

High-end servers perform very specific jobs, and that their designs always require fault-free operation - the server is not expected to crash at all.

### Server roles

The minimum specification for a server hardware would depend largely on the role the server is going to play, the processes and services that will run on it, and the number of users it will have. Also note that a server can be configured to perform specific roles. The applications that the server runs determine the particular server's role. For a server to undertake a role, additional services and features will have to be installed. This is why the server's role is the single most important factor in determining the hardware that a server requires. Typical server roles include:

- Backup server
- Database server
- Domain controller
- Directory Server
- File server
- Print server
- RAS server

- Web server
- Email server

Do note that in the world of Windows computing, a domain controller stores a copy of Active Directory and maintains the directory data store. Active Directory aims to provide a centralized repository of information for securely managing an organization's resources.

## Windows Server Operating Systems Overview

An operating system is the most important program that runs on a computer. Every computer must have an operating system to run other programs. It performs all the basic tasks, such as recognizing input from the keyboard, sending output to the display screen, keeping track of files and directories on the disk, and controlling peripheral devices of all kinds. Server operating system differs from a desktop one in that it is often optimized for handling processes that run behind the scenes (the background processes).

MS classifies Windows Server 2008 editions into "general" purpose editions and special purpose editions. Talking about the general purpose editions, Windows Server 2008 R2 Datacenter is said to deliver enterprise-class platform for deploying business-critical applications and large-scale virtualization on small and large servers. Windows Server 2008 R2 Enterprise is intended to act as an advanced server platform that provides cost-effective and reliable support for mission-critical workloads. Windows Server 2008 R2 Standard is the entry level Windows Server operating system with built-in enhanced Web and virtualization capabilities.

Talking about the special purpose editions, Windows Web Server 2008 R2 uses Internet Information Services IIS 7.5 and serves exclusively as an Internet-facing server. Windows Server 2008 R2 for Itanium-Based Systems aims to deliver enterprise-class platform for deploying business-critical applications running on Itanium based systems. Windows Server 2008 R2 Foundation is an entry level edition designed specifically for small businesses which restricts the number of concurrent remote desktop services connections and is able to use only one processor. Do remember, Windows Web Server can become a member of an Active Directory domain but cannot be configured to serve as a domain controller. FYI, if you want to install .NET Framework 3.0 on Windows Server 2008 R2 you MUST also install IIS. Both are not installed by default.

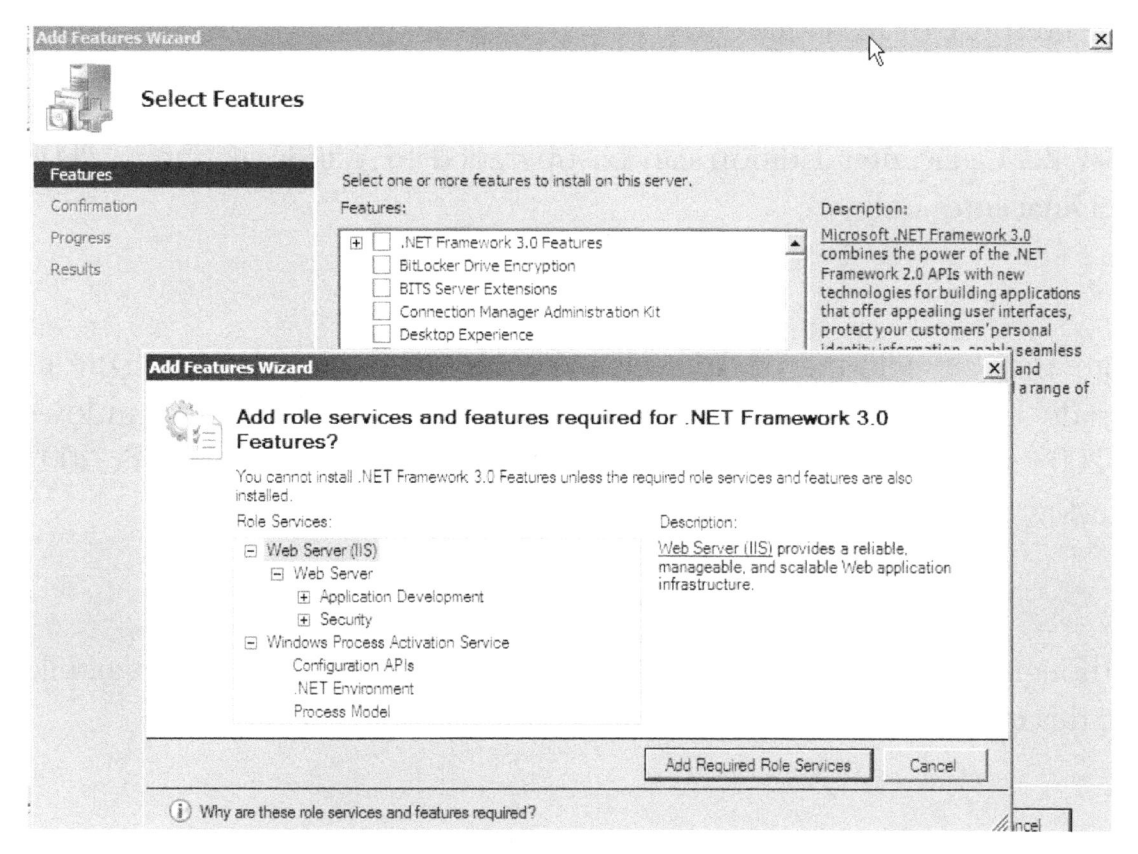

You want to know that in-place upgrades from 32-bit to 64-bit architectures are never supported. Keep in mind that all R2 editions are 64-bit only! In-place upgrades from one language to another are also not possible. If your concern is on possible upgrade from 2003 Server to 2008 R2, note that:

- Windows Server 2003 Standard Edition with SP2 or Windows Server 2003 R2 Standard Edition can be upgraded to Windows Server 2008 R2 Standard or R2 Enterprise

- Windows Server 2003 Enterprise Edition with SP2 or Windows Server 2003 R2 Enterprise Edition can be upgraded to Windows Server 2008 R2 Enterprise or R2 Datacenter

- Windows Server 2003 Datacenter Edition with SP2 or Windows Server 2003 R2 Datacenter Edition can be upgraded to Windows Server 2008 R2 Datacenter only

Do note that all editions of Windows Server 2008 include the right to downgrade – you may choose to downgrade to lesser editions of Windows Server 2008 as well as equivalent or lesser editions of Windows Server 2003 R2, Windows Server 2003 …etc.

Even though Windows Server 2012 has been released for quite awhile already, this exam does not cover 2012 for now.

A Server Core installation option allows the installing of Windows Server 2008 R2 with a minimal environment for running specific server roles. The environment has no GUI and everything is done at the command prompt. This is supposed to be able to cut down the maintenance and management requirements as well as the attack surface for those server roles. Possible server roles in this format are:

- Active Directory Certificate Services
- Active Directory Domain Services
- Active Directory Lightweight Directory Services (AD LDS)
- DHCP Server
- DNS Server
- File Services (including File Server Resource Manager)
- Hyper-V
- Print and Document Services
- Streaming Media Services
- Web Server

A full blown server has a different set of roles and are configurable through the Add Roles Wizard of Server Manager. A server computer can have multiple roles.

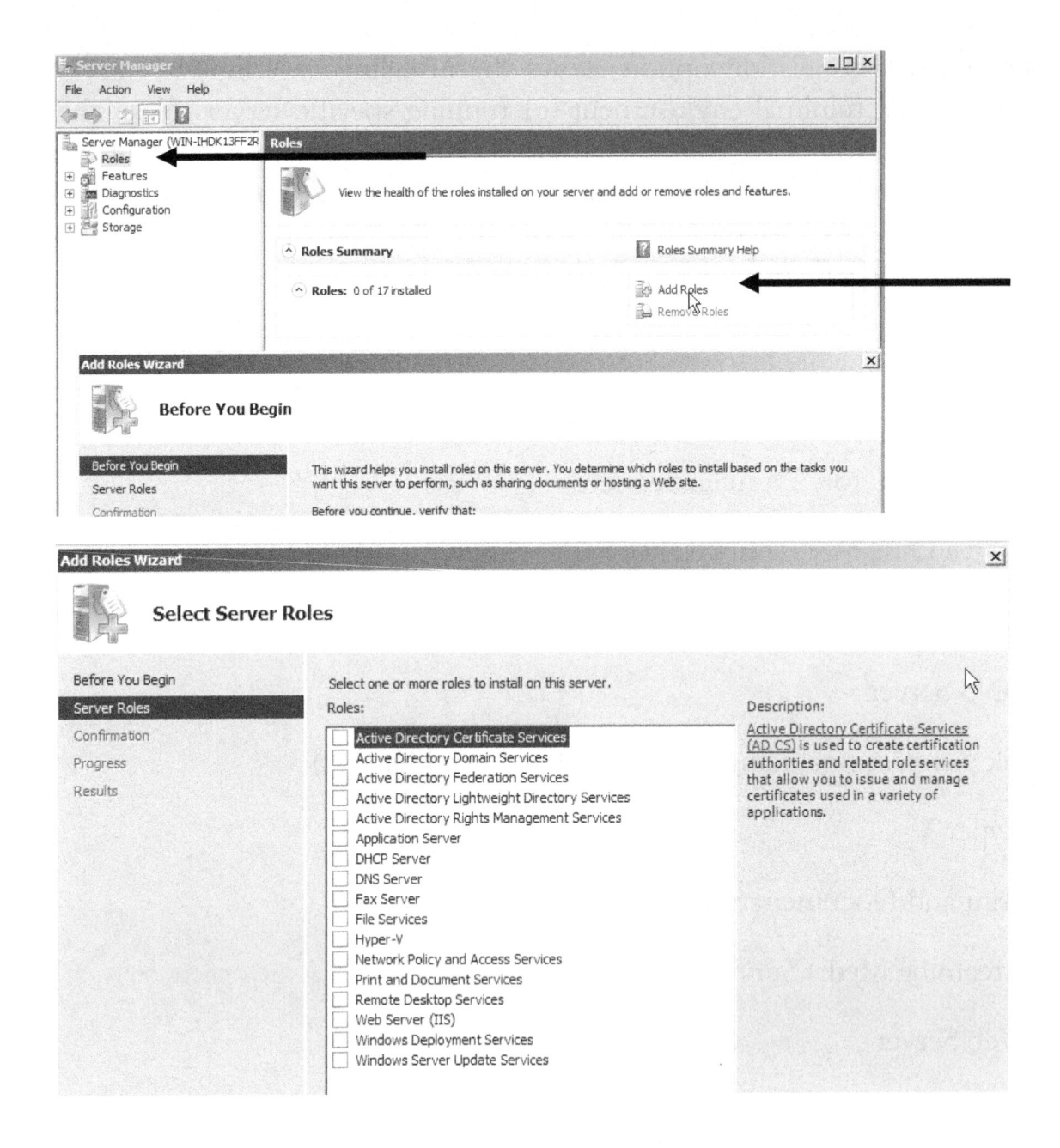

## File System and Partitions

A file system is a data structure that an operating system uses to keep track of files on a disk or partition. Windows Servers 2008 R2 is still NTFS based, with two new features. Transactional NTFS allows file operations to be performed in a transactional manner, with support for full atomic, consistent, isolated, and durable semantics for transactions. Self-healing NTFS can correct disk file corruptions online without requiring Chkdsk.exe to be run by hand. A directory represents the way the files are organized on the disk. You can think of the file system as a hierarchical collection of files and directories that make up an organized, structured set of stored information you can retrieve if needed or wanted. You should create folders when you want to organize your data into groups and to store data hierarchically on the hard disk. For example, if you wanted to store photos, you may want to create a folder on your hard disk called MY BEAUTIFUL PHOTOS and store all of them in there. You may want to go further and create subdirectories to store groupings within this like one folder for LOVER and another for SCENES.

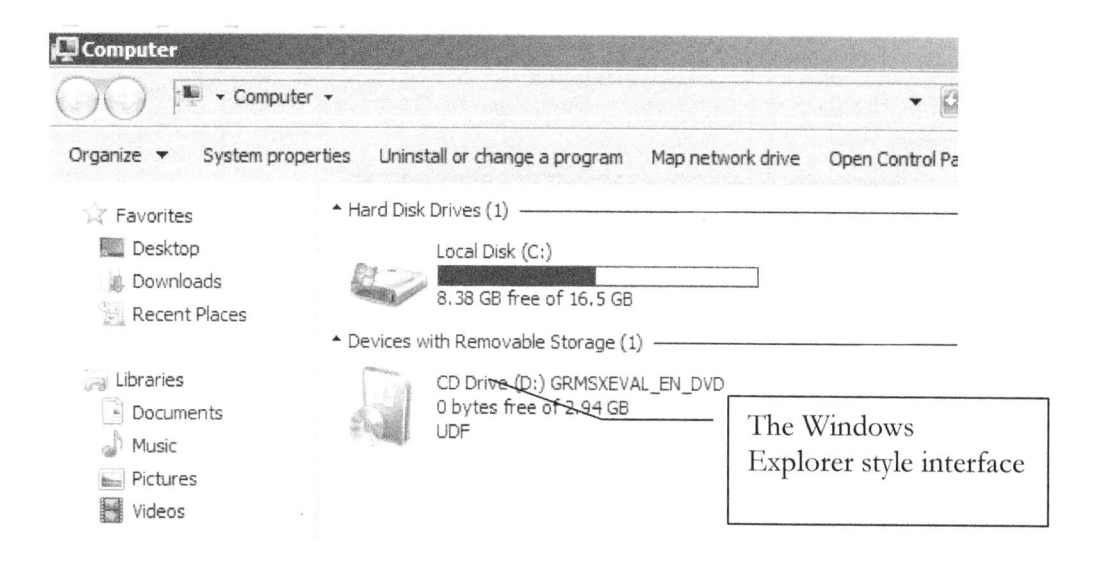

The Windows Explorer style interface

Windows Explorer is the Windows Shell interface to the desktop and filing system. It is split into two panes with a collapsible hierarchy showing the directory structure on the left side, and a sub window displaying the current folder's contents at the right. The Computer Manager, on the other hand, is where all your computer management tools reside within a convenient interface. Inside there is the Disk Management Console.

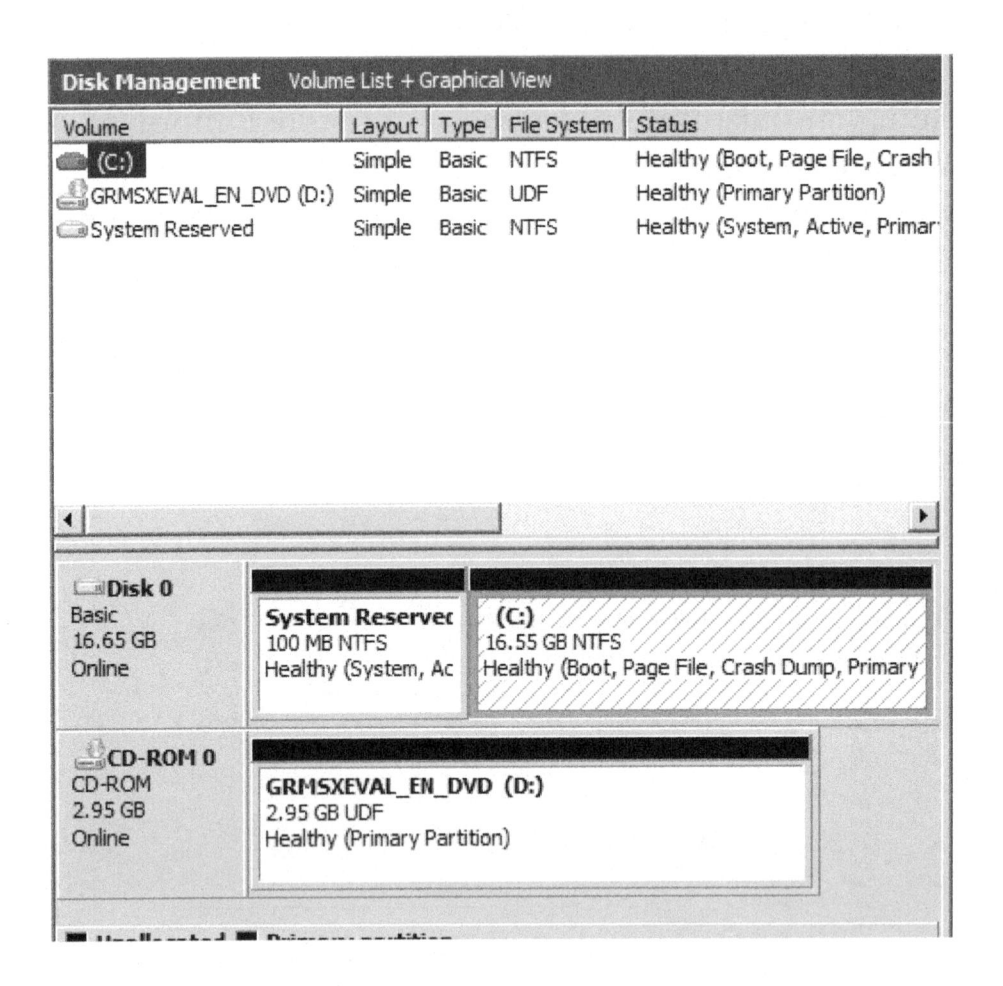

Partitioning refers to the process of creating virtual markers that separate drive letters in DOS and Windows. There are 3 types of partitions: primary, extended & logical. A partition table is the list of what partitions have been configured on a drive. The Disk Defragmenter can consolidate fragmented files and folders on your computer's hard disk, so that each occupies a single, contiguous space on the volume. As a result, your system can gain access to your files and folders and save new ones more efficiently. The backup and restore utility (and other disaster recovery utilities) can help you keep your data safe. If you have a disk failure, if you accidentally delete data, the backup and restore utility can help you to get back on track.

On the other hand, the Disk Cleanup Wizard can check a specified volume and estimates the amount of disk space it might be able to recover and let you use once completed. Attrib is a command line utility that can be used to view or alter file permissions, including A: Archive; R: Read Only; S: System; and H: Hidden.

## SMP and multi-core processors

Symmetric multiprocessing SMP is the kind of multiprocessor computer architecture which allows for two or more identical processors connected to a single shared main memory (remember those boards that let you plug in more than one CPUs?). Most multiprocessor systems today use a SMP architecture. Because they share the same main memory, bottleneck can still occur in the coordination of resources.

In the case of multi-core processors*, the SMP architecture works at the cores, effectively treating them as separate processors in the same die. This technology is particularly popular in the PC market where cost of manufacturing is a major concern. Alternative architectures include asymmetric multiprocessing in which separate specialized processors are put in place for specific tasks, and computer clustered multiprocessing in memory availability to processors are specifically assigned.

To enjoy the benefits offered by these processors your OS must be capable of doing so (for example, multithreading may have to be supported, which allows application processes to be run in parallel). For PC level computers and servers, certain Windows Server editions can support SMP/multicore processors without any manual modification.

*A multi-core CPU (sometimes known as a chip-level multiprocessor) is a relatively new kind of CPU technology which combines two or more independent processor cores into a single die. For the PC market there are dual core processors as well as quad core processors being offered at pretty affordable price levels.*

With a dual-core configuration, an integrated circuit has two complete computer processors included together. These identical processors are placed side by side on the same die, each with its own path heading towards the system front-side bus. Multi-core is simply an expansion to the dual-core concept. Do realize that optimization for the dual-core processor architecture would require both the operating system and the software applications to support thread-level parallelism TLP. This technology allows things to be done simultaneously.

## Processors and Licensing

You need to know the concept of processor units due to hardware specifications and licensing. Standard edition is limited to four processors and can accept no more than 250 concurrent connections for its Routing and Remote Access Service, which is typically sufficient for a branch office setup.

Enterprise does not have any connection limits and can support up to eight processors. Datacenter edition can support up to 64 processors and allows for hot replacement of memory and processors. It requires one license per physical processor in the server machine. Itanium edition is also licensed on a per-processor basis.

Microsoft's licensing rules generally preclude casual reassignment of Windows Server licenses from one physical server system to another. Simply put, Server licenses may not be reassigned too frequently.

In addition to server licenses on the server systems, all editions of Windows Server other than the Web Edition require clients to be licensed with either Client Access Licenses or External Connectors (those with Windows Server External Connector license). Also, Terminal Services requires its own client licenses, that the typical CAL and External Connector license would not give rights to using Terminal Services.

## 64 bit Computing and Memory Support

Modern servers are almost all 64-bit based. A 64-bit architecture can in theory more than double the amount of data a CPU can process on a per clock cycle basis. A performance increase is usually visible since a 64-bit CPU can handle more memory and larger files. In fact, a 64-bit architecture can allow a server to address way more RAM. With 32 bit, 4GB is max.

Windows Server 2008 R2 Datacenter can use max 2 TB of RAM. Windows Server 2008 R2 Enterprise and Windows Server 2008 R2 for Itanium-Based Systems can also use max 2 TB of RAM. Windows Server 2008 R2 Foundation can support max 8 GB. Windows Server 2008 R2 Standard can go up to 32 GB. Windows HPC Server 2008 R2 can support 128 GB. Windows Web Server 2008 R2 can use only 32 GB max.

Do remember, benefits of a 64-bit architecture can be realized only if you are running a 64-bit operating system and 64-bit software and drivers. 32-bit software running on a 64bit platform will not go any faster.

Windows Server 2008 R2 and later are all 64bit only. The focus of this exam is on R2, which is technologically more advance than the original 2008!

**Virtualization, Hyper-V and Licensing**

With Virtualization technologies a single physical device can act like having multiple physical versions of itself for sharing across the network. This is usually done with the help of multiple processor cores in the same processor die. Platform virtualization is performed by the host software. As a control program, this host creates a simulated computer environment for formulating a virtual machine to serve the guest software. With full virtualization, the virtual machine will simulate sufficient hardware functionality to allow an unmodified OS to run in isolation. On the other hand, with paravirtualization the virtual machine will not simulate hardware but will simply offer a special API to serve those modified guest OS.

Hyper-V is a server role that provides tools and services one can use to create a virtualized server computing environment. This feature requires an x64-based processor, hardware-assisted virtualization, and hardware data execution prevention DEP. It can run on Standard, Enterprise, and Datacenter editions. You add this role via Server Manager - Add Roles. You create a new virtual machine via Administrative Tools - Hyper-V Manager.

You can also create virtual networks on the server running Hyper-V for use with the various virtual machines and virtualization server. An external network provides communication between a virtual machine and a physical network. An internal network provides communication between the virtualization server and virtual machines. A private network provides communication between virtual machines. All these can be configured via the Hyper-V Manager -> Virtual Network Manager.

You can also add Hyper-V to a server core installation but you will need to use dism for this. The command is Dism /online /enable-feature /featurename:Microsoft-Hyper-V.

The main concern on virtualization related licensing is that server licenses for all editions of Windows Server are assigned to physical servers only. However, any server system running Windows Server in a virtual machine must still be licensed. In fact, even if you use a third-party virtualization technology you will still need to buy Windows Server licenses for the server.

## Cloud Computing

Cloud computing is all about distributed computing. An application is built using resources from multiple services from the same or different locations. By knowing the endpoint to access the services, the user can use software as a service, much like utility computing. Behind the scene there are grids of computers and the user does not need to know the details of the background stuff.

Grid computing describes the act of sharing tasks over multiple computers. A computational grid works by applying the resources of multiple computers together to resolving a single problem. A private cloud is a cloud computing infrastructure operated solely for a single organization. **In any case, cloud computing is energy friendly because people are effectively sharing computing resources.**

## Hardware capacity planning

The processor speed indicates the speed at which a processor can complete a certain amount of cycles per second. One Hertz means one cycle completed in a second. One megahertz means one million cycles completed in a second. One gigahertz means one billion cycles completed per second. This is now the most popular processor speed measurement unit. **Officially, all versions of Windows Server 2008 R2 require at least a 1.4 GHz 64-bit processor, 512MB of RAM, and minimum 32 GB drive space. Practically, these minimums do not make sense and you want to use hardware with way better specifications!**

Server load is almost always driven by peak users. Practically, server load is difficult to predict so live testing would be the best way to determine the hardware capacity required. Server hardware can almost always benefit from having more RAM. This is due to the fact that as soon as the operating system has to write data onto the drive the server will experience a performance drop. The choice of processor, on the other hand, is usually dependant on how intensively the server is used. The nature of workload has to be considered too. For example, a file server will not require anywhere near the same processor power as a database server since file access doesn't require much computation; it does require faster I/O.

## Storage capacity planning

In terms of storage, SCSI disks are reliable, and that most of them have the ability to mark bad sectors as unreadable via the SCSI adaptors disk utilities. HOWEVER, they are very expensive. SATA and PATA hard drives are cheaper but are less reliable when under high workload.

Talking about speed, traditional SCSI technology (all the way up to SCSI-3 standard) does not really keep up with the serial technologies being developed for PC. SAS Serial Attached SCSI is a newer SCSI standard with a much higher transfer speed (6Gb/sec or so).

A RAID configuration can provide additional protection against data loss by mirroring the data on multiple hard disks, thus protecting yourself from disk failure. The more disks a server has the better the redundancy. Hardware RAID generally performs better than software RAID since hardware RAID has a dedicated chip for managing the RAID operation. Windows Server natively supports software RAID. RAID 0 has two disks. Data is distributed to two disks for taking advantage of higher disk read/write speeds. If one disk fails, there is no way you can recover the data. RAID 1 also has two disks. Data is written to two disks so if one disk fails you still have an exact copy on the other. RAID 5 has three disks minimum. The disks keep both data and parity information. If any one disk fails, it can be replaced and the data can be recovered.

In Windows Server 2008 R2, everything related to the management of the disk systems can be performed through the Disk Management console. You can also use it to create software RAID configurations. Diskpart can also achieve the same but doing this via the command line can be complicated.

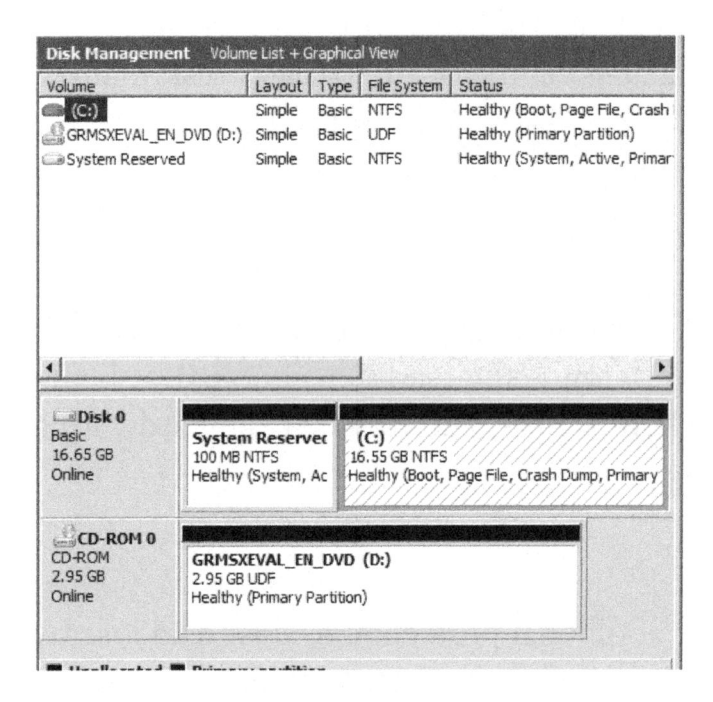

A RAID 1 mirror set can be created via the New Mirrored Volume wizard. You need to have 2 disks for it. A RAID 5 implementation, on the other hand, requires at least 3 disk drives. You use the New RAID-5 Volume wizard to configure it. You highlight a partition and right click on it then you will see the needed options. Another important function is the ability to shrink an active volume. You won't lose any data after this operation assuming you have done things correctly.

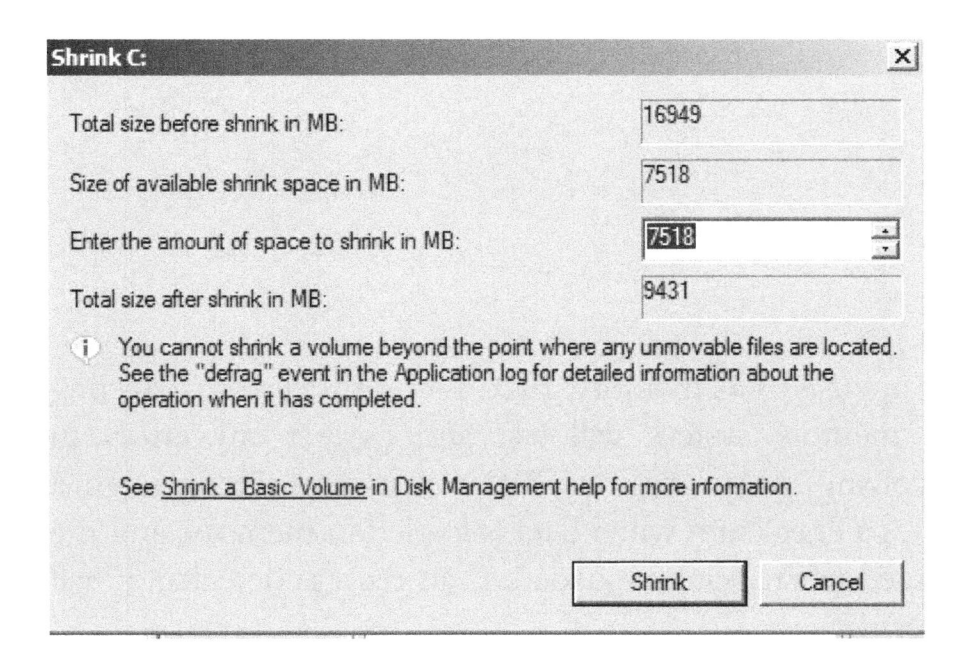

A NAS network-attached storage is a server dedicated to file sharing and nothing else. A SAN Storage Area Network, on the other hand, is a high-speed network of shared storage devices which is available to all servers on the network. FCIP Fibre Channel over IP is a new network storage technology that combines the features of Fibre Channel and IP for connecting distributed SANs over long distances. It is in fact a tunneling protocol capable of providing congestion control and management.

Windows Server 2008 R2 has a tool called the Storage Explorer which helps in managing these new SAN storage technologies.

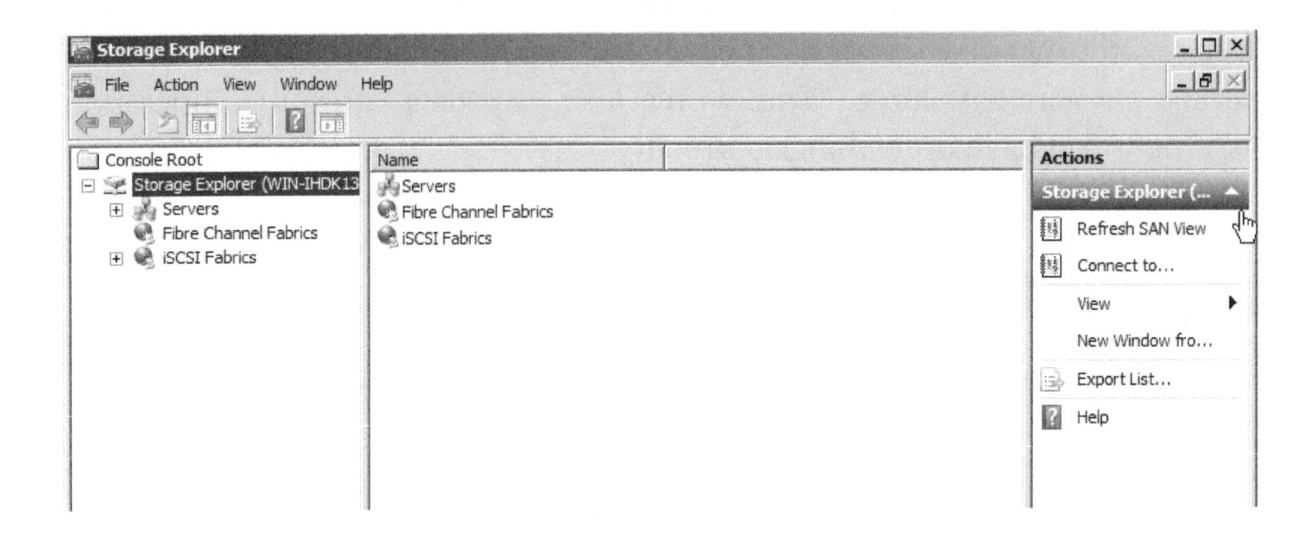

Advanced servers always use ECC memory. ECC memory is error correcting code memory. This memory system will test and correct any errors in memory without involving the processor. The way it works is through a checksum - it generates a checksum when data is loaded in memory, and the checksum is recomputed when being unloaded. If an error is detected, it will be automatically corrected.

## Load balancing

One way to achieve server scalability is to have more servers added to the configuration so to distribute the load among the group of servers (server cluster). The load distribution among these servers is what we call load balancing. When there are multiple servers in a server group, network traffic needs to be evenly distributed among the servers.

Round Robin Load Balancing is primarily for DNS service. There is a built-in round robin feature of the BIND DNS server. It works by cycling through the IP addresses corresponding to a server group. Hardware load balancers are dedicated for routing TCP/IP packets to various servers in a cluster. They are more efficient and way costlier. Software Load Balancers are usually options that come shipped with expensive server application packages. Software based solutions usually cost less but are often application specific.

**Server performance monitoring, maintenance and tuning**

To troubleshoot performance problems you must monitor - that is, to track down the problem using the available monitoring resources. If you do not monitor, you will have no way solving the problem. To achieve the best possible performance, you need to identify the performance bottlenecks and minimize the time it takes for the server to process user requests. Generally, you need to:

- monitor memory and CPU usage

- resolve hardware or software issues that may be causing problems - sometimes it is a hardware problem. Sometimes it may be a software one...

- before you start monitoring, first establish baseline performance metrics for the server by measuring server performance at various times and under different load conditions so proper comparison can be made.

A comprehensive monitoring plan should cover these:

- what server resources should be monitored
- what filter to use for reducing the amount of information collected
- what performance counters to use for watching resource usage
- what data to log

Generally speaking, these are what you should watch for:

- Memory Usage - you want to know the amount of memory the services need relative to themselves and to the operating system memory. Both your operating system and your services should have sufficient memory to use.
- CPU usage - high CPU utilization rates means the processor is underpowered.
- Disk I/O performance - when there is too much I/O you may need to add more RAM and at the same time upgrade to a high performance disk system
- Blocking Locks - this happens when a process keeps another from accessing the resource. This is often a problem specific to the service in use.

If you are using Windows, these are the tools you can use to monitor:

- Performance Monitor
- Access logs
- Event logs

Periodic maintenance on server systems are preventive measures that are mandatory due to the possible needs for:

- Installation of patches
- Hardware upgrades
- Software patches and upgrades
- Software and component installations
- Re-configurations
- Server reboots
- Availability testing

These are the common server maintenance tasks:

- Check disk space usage
- Clean out temporary files

- Update Antivirus and Anti-Spyware software
- Check backup of system state
- Check all scheduled tasks
- Check local daily backup to external hard disk
- Check daily web based backup if any
- Check e-mail mailbox usage
- Check event logs
- Check surge protectors and UPS systems
- Check weekly drive imaging if any

**Server troubleshooting**

The first step in server troubleshooting is to identify the environment in which the problem occurred. This may include both the hardware and software versions as well as any currently applied patches.

You should know the operating system version and most recently applied patches for each of the systems involved, as well as their security details. Additionally, you need to figure out the version and patch level of any additional software packages that are interacting with your server. In many cases, errors are the results of missing service pack or outdated operating system level.

With sufficient information on hand, you now have to clearly identify the actual problem. Your focuses should be on addressing these:

- What had happened
- Where…
- When…
- What effect it had on the server and the computing environment

Then you need to identify the full scope of the problem. To do so you need to detect a behavioral pattern for the problem. Ask yourself these questions:

- How many servers or components are experiencing the error?
- What is the impact of a single error?
- How many errors on each server or component?
- What is the total impact?
- Can the problem be reproduced in a test environment?
- Does the problem recur periodically?
- Has the problem spread to other components or servers?

After identifying the problem and scope, it is time to identify the potential cause(s). The key question to ask - what changes have been made to the server recently?

Once you have picked and applied a solution, make sure you verify that it is a viable solution and not just a temporary fix. You don't attack just the symptom. You need to attack the root cause of the problem. If you can confirm that you have identified the true cause, then you should identify steps to eliminate the potential for a repeat of that problem.

## Special considerations

Generally speaking, when implementing servers you want to anticipate the factors of performance, cost, reliability as well as ownership and responsibility. Performance may best be characterized by response time. Cost wise you want to minimize the number of servers. You do want your servers to be reliable. If possible they should be placed near the local support resources. Note that IT organizations usually place the backbone servers in data centers with proper environmental controls, uninterrupted power supplies, and a 24-hour support team. Locating critical server resources in a controlled environment can isolate the servers from external threats and can shorten the time necessary to recover from sudden failure.

## Network Infrastructure and Basic Windows Networking

A typical top down approach to network infrastructure design requires that you understand the constraints and objectives of network use as well as the applications and data on which your business relies upon on, before considering the viable tech options. It is therefore advisable that you start with the business objectives because your network has the most important mission of helping end users in achieving their business objectives.

Server Message Block SMB is the protocol deployed by Windows for file sharing and other communications. It serves as the basis for NetBIOS communications and resources sharing over the network. SMB traffic stays in LAN only.

Share permissions apply only when a user is accessing a file or folder non-locally. They can be applied on a user or on a group level, although assigning permissions on a group basis is always recommended. Individual permissions and group permissions can be combined to form the user's effective permissions. NTFS permissions allow you to assign permissions more granularly at the folder and file level while Share permissions are limited to the folder level only. Keep in mind, file permissions always take precedence over folder permissions.

Event Viewer is the interface for managing event logging in Windows. The primary types of log are System logs, Application logs and Security logs. It is always advised that you focus on monitoring failed login/access attempts.

Single sign-on SSO refers to the kind of access control method which enables a user to authenticate once and gain access to network resources of other software systems. Kerberos is an authentication protocol in use by the newer Windows Servers (since Windows 2000) for facilitating the implementation of SSO.

SNMP is deployed by many network management systems for monitoring network-attached devices for conditions that warrant administrative attention. The SNMP protocol itself does not define which information a managed system should offer. Instead, it relies on the various management information bases MIBs to do the job. The Microsoft SMS System Management Server makes extensive use of SNMP. The community string serves as kind of a "password" for SNMP communication. Do note that the use of SNMP will increase network load quite a bit.

On a Windows network with Active Directory enabled, information necessary for authentication is stored in the directory – that is, each Domain Controller holds a copy – information is replicated across the entire network domain. If you have multiple domain controllers up and running, server failure would not disrupt authentication unless all domain controllers within a domain fail altogether.

**Open System Interconnect**

It offers a 7 layer model which can be used as a guideline for systematic network design, management and troubleshooting.

- The Application Layer is responsible for identifying and establishing the availability of desired communication partner and verifying sufficient resources exist for communication.

- The Presentation Layer is responsible for presenting the data in standard formats and provides services such as data compression, decompression, encryption, and decryption.

- The Session Layer is responsible for coordinating communication between network nodes.

- The Transport Layer is responsible for flow control, with the primary aim of maintaining data integrity. Simply put, it works to ensure complete data transfer.

- The Network Layer has the primary responsibility of sending data packets from the source network to the destination network using a pre-specified routing method.

- The Data Link Layer is divided into the sub-layers of Logical Link Control (LLC) and Media Access Control (MAC). The LLC sub-layer handles tasks such as error control, flow control and framing, while the MAC sub-layer handles access to shared media.

- The Physical Layer allows the actual flow of signals.

- Routing takes place at layer 3. On the other hand, switching takes place at layer 2. Routing requires more complicated configuration (usually).

## Routing and switching

TCP/IP is the communication language of internet networking devices. It requires routing in order to reach the outside networks. In other words, you need to use router to connect different networks together. Routing table is the major element required for making routing decision by the routers. Main considerations while building this routing table may include Administrative distance and Metrics amidst others.

Routing protocols are for routers to communicate with each others. Routing Information Protocol RIP is an example of routing protocol. It is a distance-vector routing protocol which uses information provided to it by its neighboring routers to maintain information in a routing table on the cost of routing entries, measured in the units of hops and other metrics. A routed protocol contains the actual data elements. It can be routed by a router. TCP/IP itself is a routed protocol.

RIP for dynamic routing configuration is easy to setup but offers poor scalability as it's mechanism is limited by hop counts (the route with the fewest number of hops is always the best route), thus is mostly for LAN use. OSPF is better for large network due to a more sophisticated mechanism (it determines the best route by taking into account bandwidth as well as other factors) but is more complicated to set up. BGP is strictly a routing protocol for WAN.

Technically a Windows Server is acting as a router if it has multiple network interfaces connecting to different network segments. It supports routing protocols such as RIP (version 2).

**IP Addressing**

To build and run a large network, you will have to take care of IP addresses subnet configuration and possibly routing table configuration. You may as well want to deploy routing protocols. This holds true for both LAN and WAN.

An IP address is the unique number ID assigned to one network interface. It is 32 bit based (as per IPv4). A subnet is a portion of a network sharing a particular subnet address. The gateway address is the router's address. In a Class A address, the first octet is the network portion. In a Class B address, the first two octets are the network portion. In a Class C address, the first three octets are the network portion. Multicast IP addresses are Class D IP addresses ranging from 224.0.0.0 to 239.255.255.255.

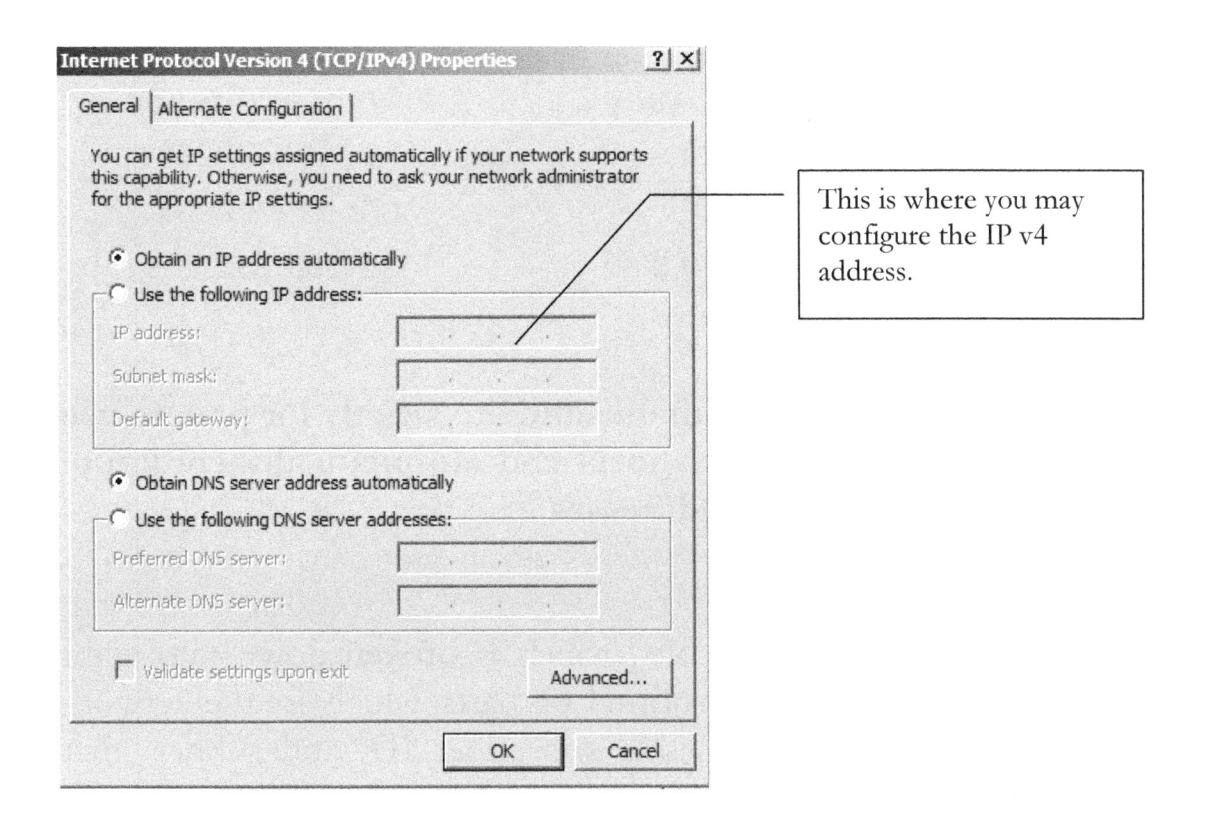

This is where you may configure the IP v4 address.

You want to know the address ranges:

| IP V4 Address Classes | Leftmost bits | Start range | End range |
|---|---|---|---|
| A | 0xxx | 0.0.0.0 | 127.255.255.255 |
| B | 10xx | 128.0.0.0 | 191.255.255.255 |
| C | 110x | 192.0.0.0 | 223.255.255.255 |
| D | 1110 | 224.0.0.0 | 239.255.255.255 |
| E | 1111 | 240.0.0.0 | 255.255.255.255 |

Class D addresses are for multicast, while class E addresses are reserved. 255.255.255.255 is a limited broadcast address. 127.0.0.1 is the loopback address for testing purpose. Also note that these are the private address ranges (for use internally without capabilities of internet access):

| V4 Classes | Private start range | Private end range |
|---|---|---|
| A | 10.0.0.0 | 10.255.255.255 |
| B | 172.16.0.0 | 172.31.255.255 |
| C | 192.168.0.0 | 192.168.255.255 |

**Private IP addresses are non-routable and are strictly for private use inside a private network. Many hosts can automatically configure their IP settings to use private addresses.**

The IPv6 address space has 128 bits, which is broken down into eight groups of 16 bits. There are two major 64-bit parts, which are the network prefix (contains the registry, provider, subscriber ID, and subnet) that occupies the higher order groups of bits and the interface ID that occupies the lower bits.

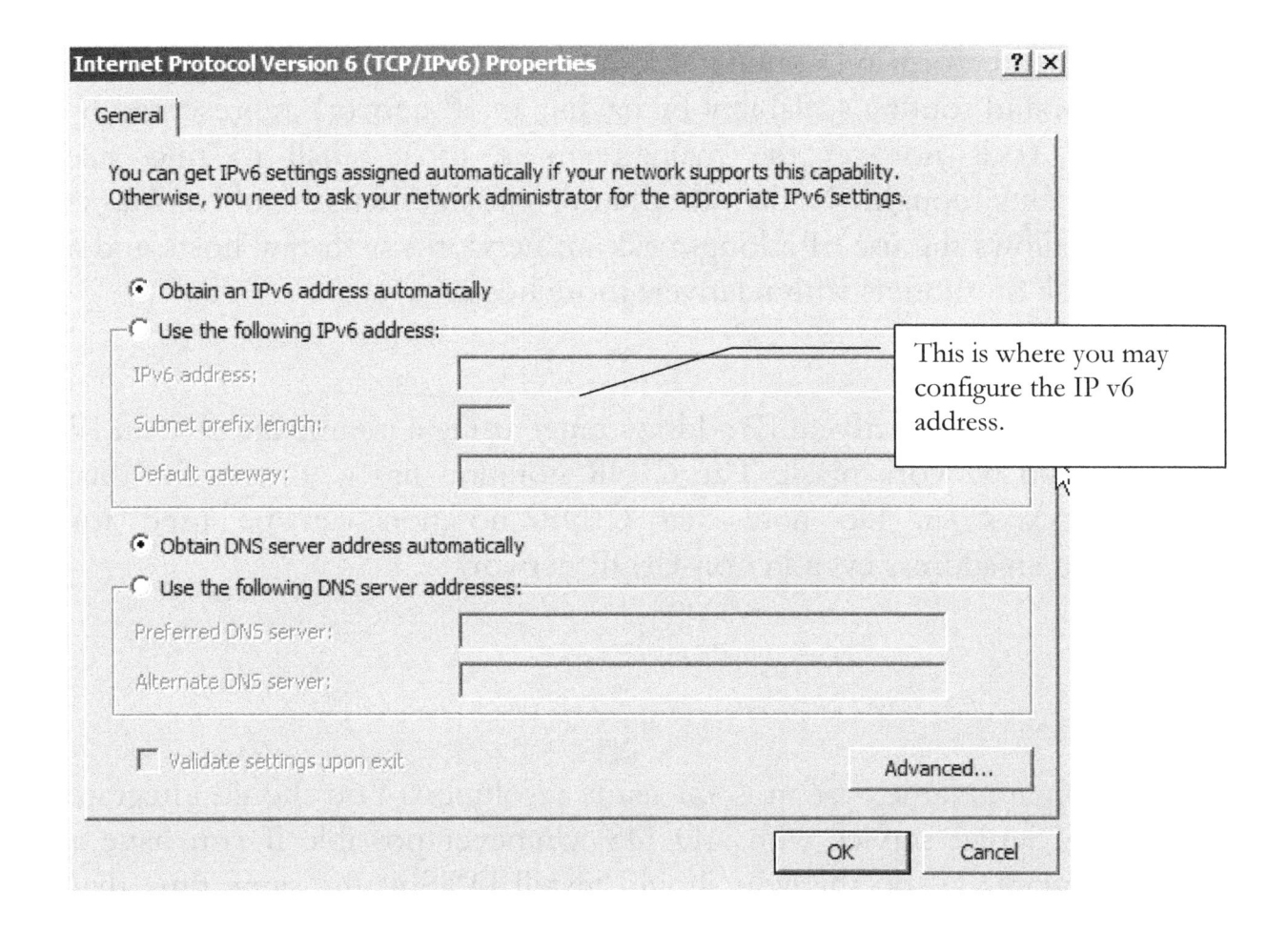

*Screenshot: Internet Protocol Version 6 (TCP/IPv6) Properties dialog with a callout "This is where you may configure the IP v6 address." pointing to the IPv6 address fields.*

## Server 2008 R2 supports both IPV4 and IPV6 addressing natively.

## IP subnetting

A subnet mask has four bytes thus totaling 32 bits. It is often written using the dotted-decimal notation, with the leftmost bits always set to the value of 1. Network hosts on different subnets are only allowed to communicate through routers (regular switches won't do the tricks). By applying a subnet mask to an IP address you effectively split the address into two parts, the first being an extended network address and the second being a host address.

Classless Interdomain Routing CLDR improves both address space utilization and routing scalability by having an IP network represented by a prefix. It is not yet the mainstream in most small to mid size environments though. On the other hand, Variable Length Subnet Masks (VLSM) allows the use of a long mask on networks with few hosts and a short mask on subnets with relatively more hosts.

With CIDR, you specify an IP address range using a combination of an IP address and network mask. The CIDR notation has a format like this: xxx.xxx.xxx.xxx/n. Do note that CIDR notation can be used for specifying an address even in non-CIDR networks.

## DNS

DNS Domain Name System is for name resolution. You should integrate the DNS Server service with AD DS whenever possible if you have a large network. To do this you should install DNS at the same time that you install AD DS, or install DNS after you install AD DS and then integrate DNS as a separate step. 2008 Server R2 based DNS servers can return both IPv4 host (A) resource records and IPv6 host (AAAA) resource records in response to queries.

DNS performs name-to-IP mapping per the request of the client devices. The DNS namespace must be planned. A common practice is to have one namespace for the internal network and another for external contact. When a new DNS server is not to serve also as a domain controller, you may configure it by first creating a forward and reverse (this is optional) lookup zone, then decide if the server is to allow dynamic updates and whether queries will be forwarded to other servers. You can choose to designate a DNS server on your local network as a forwarder by configuring the forwarding of queries so you may manage name resolution for names that belong to the outside world. A conditional forwarder is one that forwards DNS queries according to the DNS domain name involved. In other words, only some but not all queries will be forwarded.

Windows 2008 R2 based DNS Server service supports incremental zone transfers between servers that need to replicate zone data. This can greatly reduce DNS replication traffic. Directory-integration is preferred since dynamic updates to DNS will be sent to any AD DS-integrated DNS server and will get replicated to all other AD DS-integrated DNS servers via AD DS replication, which is more efficient and reliable. Also, it is possible to use access control list to secure the relevant object container in the directory tree. Because zones will get replicated and synchronized to new domain controllers automatically whenever new installations are introduced, administration will be much easier.

It is very common to install DNS servers on all domain controllers. Generally, it is wise to place these DNS servers at a network location that is centrally accessible to the DNS clients. Performance-wise, the more zones to be handled the more workload to be expected by a DNS server. And don't forget to consider the effects of zone transfer across slower WAN links!

## DHCP and LDAP

DHCP Dynamic Host Configuration Protocol is for dynamic IP address configuration. In a modern network you will need them both for ease of administration and scalability. Do note that dynamic addresses allocation is best for frequently changing network topology with a large amount of clients. If you have very few clients, static naming may be acceptable. **Static address assignment is usually preferred for servers.**

A DHCP scope refers to an administrative grouping of IP addresses. An administrator can first create a scope for each physical subnet, then uses the scope to further define the parameters to be used by the clients. A scope has a range of IP addresses, a subnet mask and a scope name. DHCP scope options are configured for assignment to DHCP clients, such as DNS server address, router address, WINS server address, etc. Since each subnet can only have one single DHCP scope with a single continuous range of IP addresses, if you want to use multiple address ranges within a single scope then you will have to carefully configure the required exclusion ranges or conflicts will occur.

LDAP Lightweight Directory Access Protocol refers to the set of protocols for accessing information directories. It is based on the standards contained within the X.500 standard but is deliberately made simpler, so that's why it is sometimes called X.500-lite. It is an open protocol, meaning applications have no need to worry about the type of server hosting the directory.

## Wireless Based Local Area Networking

Wireless network relies on RF (Radio Frequency) to function. RF represents any frequency within the electromagnetic spectrum that is associated with radio wave propagation. Most wireless technologies for LAN use are based on RF field propagation. Potential sources of RF interference are microwave ovens, wireless phones, Bluetooth enabled devices and other wireless LANs.

A RF setup involves two parts, which are the transmitter and the receiver. The transmitter takes and encodes the message onto a sine wave for transmission. The receiver receives the radio waves and decodes accordingly. Do remember, Radio transmission ALWAYS requires a clear path between antennas (line of sight LOS).

IEEE 802.11 defines protocol for Ad-hoc and client/server networks. In particular it defines specifications for the physical layer and the Media Access Control layer. A client/server based wireless network uses an access point to control the allocation of transmit time for all wireless stations. The access point is often the target of attackers.

Wired Equivalent Privacy (WEP) is kind of a security protocol for WLAN defined in the 802.11b standard. It is not that secure though as the header and the trailer are not encrypted at all. Typical security attacks against WLANs may include Eavesdropping, RF jamming, and Encryption Cracking. The list keeps growing everyday. Wi-Fi Protected Setup (WPS) is a standard intended for the easy and secure establishment of a wireless home network. To add a new device to the wireless network there can be four choices. They are the PIN Method, the PBC Method, the NFC Method, and the USB Method. Wireless Zero Configuration (WZC) refers to Wireless Auto Configuration (WLAN AutoConfig). It is a wireless connection management utility that comes with Windows XP and later. It works by selecting a wireless network to connect to basing on a user's preferences, even in the absence of a wireless network utility from the NIC manufacturer.

## WAN Networking

A WAN covers a relatively broad geographic area that often uses transmission facilities provided by common carriers. It requires quite many different devices to run, EXAMPLES: WAN switches, access servers, modems, CSU/DSUs, and ISDN terminal adapters. A point-to-point link provides a single pre-established WAN communications path from one premise to another. You usually need to have it leased from a carrier or a service provider and thus is often called leased line.

Point-to-Point Protocol PPP is a method for connecting a computer to a remote network, over point-to-point links. It works at the data link layer, and is more stable than SLIP. Most importantly, it has error checking features included.

Many WANs deploy virtual circuits for cost sharing purpose. The two major types of virtual circuits are switched virtual circuits and permanent virtual circuits. Switched circuits allow data connections to be initiated when needed and terminated when completed. Example: ISDN. Packet switching allows users to share common carrier resources continuously without the need for connection initialization all the time. Examples include ATM, Frame Relay and X.25.

Codecs are deployed for compressing data. They are usually lossy, for achieving a relatively small file size. Lossless codecs are available, but the small increase in quality often does not worth the increase in file size. It is in fact possible to have repeated application of lossy codecs for repeated encoding and subsequent decoding, but quality will be degraded quite significantly.

## Security planning

Good network security design often follows a top down approach and must reflect the goals, characteristics, and policies of the organizations in which they operate. The primary goals that drive internetworking design and implementation are application availability, cost of ownership and user satisfaction. A top down approach to network design often calls for your understanding of the constraints and objectives of network use as well as the applications and data on which the business relies upon on, before considering the viable internetworking options.

It is always recommended that you start your design effort with the business objectives because your network has the most important mission of helping users in achieving business objectives. Once these objectives are well understood, you may proceed further. You shall gain understand on the applications that will be running on the network, the systems that are attached to the network, and the data that will be flow through them.

A proper network security design and implementation plan should outline the required network design tasks on a phase by phase, step by step manner. Within each phase there should be steps that details what are to be done. The advantage of having a proper implementation plan handy is to introduce specific network benefits according to a schedule, thus allowing for proper resource allocation, planning, change control, and configuration and installation. During the design phase, a prototype may be made available for initial testing and review. Before finalizing the new design and putting it into final production use, thorough testing must be done following a well-prepared test plan.

A proper test plan should be in place to address all the key features developed in the planning phase. It should be followed to ensure compatibility with existing system performance as well as to minimize the possibility for delay-causing problems in the deployment stage.

A packet consists of a header which marks the beginning of the packet, a payload of data, and a trailer which marks the end of the packet. The checksum if available for error checking is located at the trailer. The header has to specify the data type in transit. A firewall prevents unauthorized access to or from a private network by examining each message and/or packet that passes through it and blocks those that do not meet the specified security criteria. A packet filter examines each packet entering or leaving the network and accepts or rejects it based on pre-defined security rules. The former uses more sophisticated mechanisms and are more dynamic in nature, but is more expensive and is more costly computing resource-wise. Keep in mind, a firewall doesn't stop viruses. Boot Sector Virus attaches itself to the boot sector of a floppy disk or an executable file and copies all or part of itself onto the boot sector of your hard drive. File-Infecting Virus attaches themselves to executable files associated with other software applications. Macro Virus affects Word and Excel templates.

**Windows Server has built-in firewall support.**

## Disaster Recovery Plans For Servers

Backup copies of the operating system, the application software and all the critical data must be made on a regular basis. The frequency of the backup would depend largely on the frequency of changes made as well as the criticality of the concerned data. A backup copy of the most recent release version of the operating system and the application software should be made available during the process of rebuilding a crashed server. Backup copies of the critical data should be made available when the current data. The data should be backed up on a frequency determined by the user. Generally, application with high transaction volume should have data backups made more frequently.

There are different backup schemes for rotating and replacing backups. A backup rotation scheme refers to a method put in place for effectively backing up data where multiple media are involved in the backup process.

- A First In, First Out FIFO backup scheme involves saving the new or modified files onto the oldest media in a set. It is very simple to use.

- A Grandfather-father-son backup method has been very popular for making tape backups. It involves defining three sets of backups, which are daily (son), weekly (father) and monthly (grand father). The son backups are rotated on a daily basis with one graduating to father status every week. The father backups are rotated on a weekly basis with one graduating to grandfather status every month.

- An incremented media method has a set of numbered media that is being used until the end of the cycle. Then the cycle is repeated using media numbered the same but incremented by one.

- The Towers of Hanoi rotation method is a recursive method which is quite complex to implement.

From a technical perspective, these backup methods are available:

- The Image/block level backup method deals with blocks of data. The backup application will open the disk as a raw disk and then perform logical block-level read and write operations. Backup and restore operations are very fast but no access is allowed during the operation.

- The Application-level backup method is usually application specific. In other words, the backup and restore operations are tightly associated with the application.

- With the Differential Backup method, a differential backup will archive all changes made since the last full backup. The backup process is fast. A full backup, in contrast, is slow to backup but convenient to restore since you only need to have one set of media available.

- File-based incremental backup is typically used when a different set of files is created or modified.

- Direct-attached backup is all about attaching storage devices to the server directly. It remains a very popular topology for backing up servers.

- Network-attached backup works in a LAN. With it, you can have a server on the LAN with a backup device that could be shared by all the servers on the LAN.

- LAN-free backup assumes that a storage area network is in place to provide a high bandwidth between any two devices and offer multiple simultaneous bandwidth capability between multiple pairs of devices.

- With server-free backup, the backup server does not need to spend much effort while the actual backup is accomplished through the data mover agent - the data is moved directly from the source to the backup media without going through the backup server.

## Service packs and patches

Your OS and/or your firewall may require patching in order to stay secured. For example, Microsoft release patches to fix vulnerabilities or add security features. Patches should be applied in a consistent and repeatable manner, because failing to patch even a few computers means that the overall network is still vulnerable. Service packs typically include all the essential patching components bundled together for easy downloading. Typically, each new service pack contains all the fixes that are included in previous service packs plus any new fixes, so most of the time you would not need to install a previous service pack before you install the latest one. Do keep in mind, patches may not work perfectly in every environment. Therefore, you should thoroughly test any patches before installing in your environment. To be secure and safe, you might want to have a plan of action to restore the system to its original state if something goes wrong. Backup should be made almost mandatory in such a plan. As of the time of this writing Server 2008 has SP1 released. The link to further information and download is:

http://technet.microsoft.com/en-us/library/ff817647(v=ws.10).aspx

To avoid confusion you want to know that Windows Server 2008 and Windows Server 2008 SP2 are the same operating system at a different service pack level. Windows Server 2008 R2 is in fact the server release of Windows 7, and it is considered "newer" than Windows Server 2008 SP2. **To be precise, Windows Server 2008 is based on the 6.0 kernel, which is the same one used by Windows Vista. Windows Server**

2008 R2 is based on the 6.1 kernel, which is the one used by Windows 7.

## Questions:

1. Standard edition is limited to _____ processors and can accept no more than _____ concurrent connections for its Routing and Remote Access Service.

2. Enterprise edition can support up to _____ processors.

3. Datacenter edition can support up to _____ processors.

4. Which edition allows for hot replacement of memory and processors?

5. Itanium edition is licensed on what basis?

6. A RAID 1 mirror set can be created via what interface?

7. A RAID 5 implementation requires at least how many disk drives?

8. Describe Hyper-V. What specifications are required?

9. Windows Server 2008 R2 Datacenter can use max _____ of RAM.

10. Windows Server 2008 R2 for Itanium-Based Systems can use max _____ of RAM.

11. Windows Server 2008 R2 Foundation can support max _____ of RAM.

12. Windows Web Server 2008 R2 uses which version of Internet Information Services?

13. Windows Web Server cannot become a member of an Active Directory domain. True?

14. Windows Server 2008 R2 is based on which kernel version?

15. How do you implement in-place upgrades from 32-bit to 64-bit architectures?

16. How do you implement in-place upgrades from one language to another?

17. Windows Server 2003 Standard Edition with SP2 or Windows Server 2003 R2 Standard Edition can be upgraded to:

18. Windows Server 2003 Enterprise Edition with SP2 or Windows Server 2003 R2 Enterprise Edition can be upgraded to:

19. Describe a Server Core installation option.

## Answers:

1. *Standard edition is limited to four processors and can accept no more than 250 concurrent connections for its Routing and Remote Access Service.*

2. *Enterprise does not have any connection limits and can support up to eight processors.*

3. *Datacenter edition can support up to 64 processors.*

4. *Datacenter edition allows for hot replacement of memory and processors.*

5. *Itanium edition is licensed on a per-processor basis.*

6. *A RAID 1 mirror set can be created via the New Mirrored Volume wizard.*

7. *A RAID 5 implementation requires at least 3 disk drives.*

8. *Hyper-V is a server role that provides tools and services one can use to create a virtualized server computing environment. This feature requires an x64-based processor, hardware-assisted virtualization, and hardware data execution prevention DEP.*

9. *Windows Server 2008 R2 Datacenter can use max 2 TB of RAM.*

10. *Windows Server 2008 R2 for Itanium-Based Systems can use max 2 TB of RAM.*

11. *Windows Server 2008 R2 Foundation can support max 8 GB.*

12. *Windows Web Server 2008 R2 uses Internet Information Services IIS 7.5 and serves exclusively as an Internet-facing server.*

13. *Windows Web Server can become a member of an Active Directory domain but cannot be configured to serve as a domain controller.*

14. *Windows Server 2008 R2 is based on the 6.1 kernel, which is the one used by Windows 7.*

15. *You want to know that in-place upgrades from 32-bit to 64-bit architectures are never supported.*

16. *In-place upgrades from one language to another are not possible.*

17. *Windows Server 2003 Standard Edition with SP2 or Windows Server 2003 R2 Standard Edition can be upgraded to Windows Server 2008 R2 Standard or R2 Enterprise.*

18. *Windows Server 2003 Enterprise Edition with SP2 or Windows Server 2003 R2 Enterprise Edition can be upgraded to Windows Server 2008 R2 Enterprise or R2 Datacenter.*

19. *A Server Core installation option allows the installing of Windows Server 2008 R2 with a minimal environment for running specific server roles. The environment has no GUI and everything is done at the command prompt.*

# Overview of administrative tools and other interfaces

## Server Management UI

Generally speaking, all the essential server admin tools can be found here:

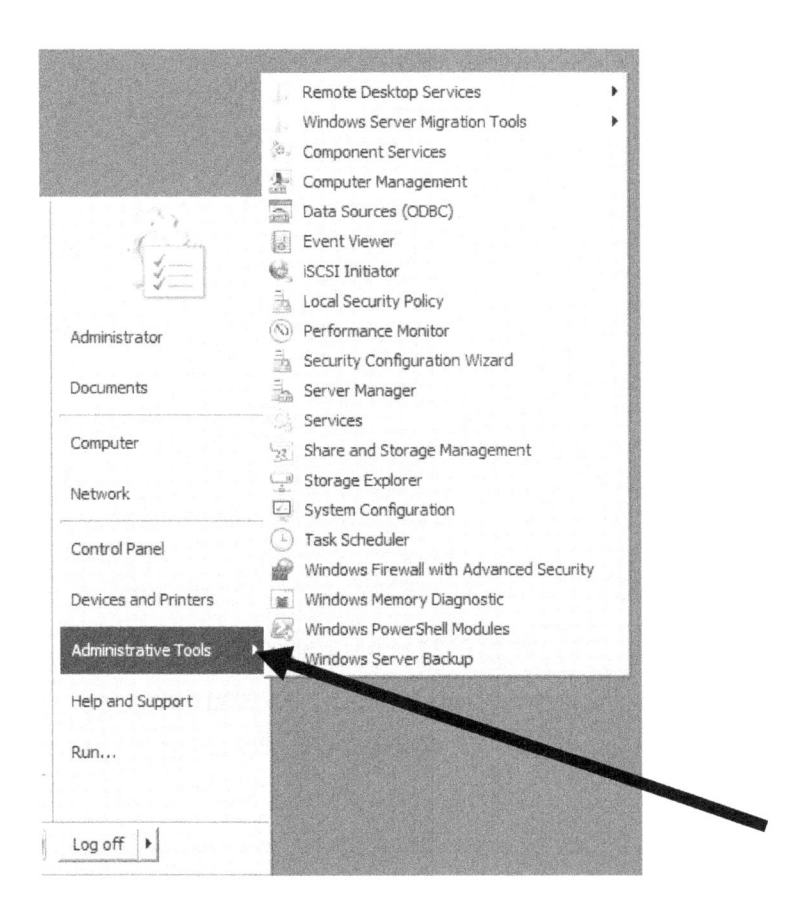

Server Manager is the primary console for server configuration and management.

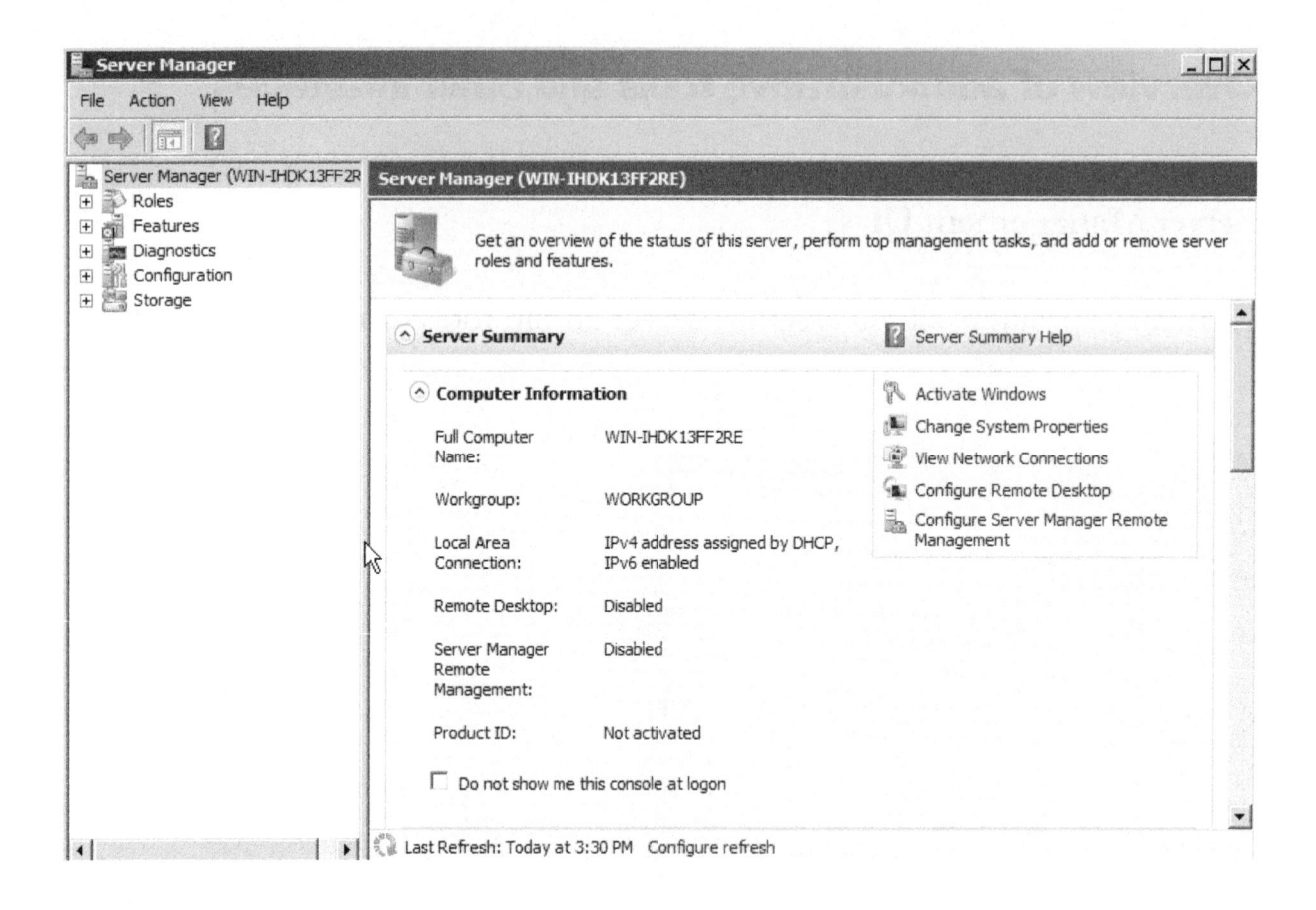

## Managing Services

The Services section lists all the available services so you can manage them from a single interface. Right click on anyone of them and there are many settings to play with. For example, you can change the startup type and the account to be used to run the service. Usually a local system account is used for logging on as a service.

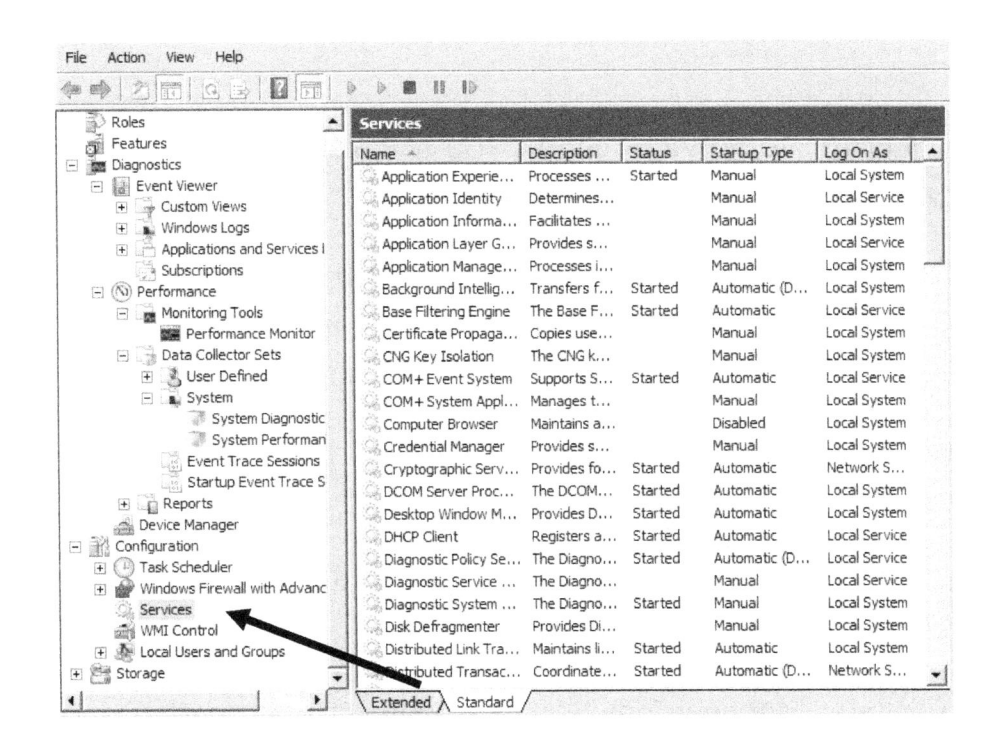

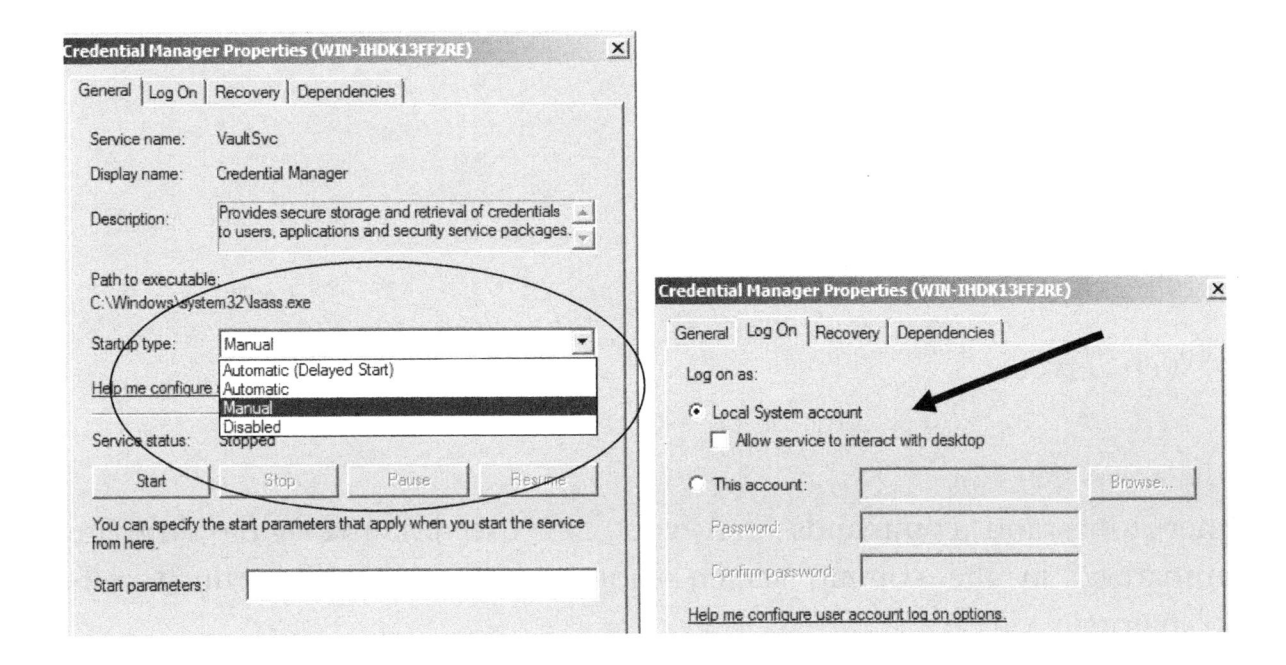

Some of the more critical services are:

55

- Active Directory Certificate Services allows you to create, distribute, and manage customized public key certificates.

- Active Directory Domain Services are responsible for storing directory data and managing communication between users and domains plus administering user logon processes.

- Active Directory Federation Services provides Web single-sign-on for authenticating web user to multiple Web applications.

- Active Directory Lightweight Directory Services provides support for directory-enabled applications.

- Active Directory Rights Management Services protects information and support AD RMS-enabled applications.

- DNS Services

- DHCP Services

- Remote Desktop Services

- File Services

- Web Server

Other tools and commands that you can use for managing AD are summarized in the coming screen shots – they are pretty much self-explanatory:

## Advanced Tools

### AD DS Tools

| Description | Tool |
|---|---|
| Administer trusts, domain and forest functional levels, and user principal name (UPN) suffixes | AD Domains and Trusts |
| Query, view, and edit objects and attributes in the directory | ADSI Edit |
| Add or remove domain controller functionality from a server using the AD DS Installation Wizard | Dcpromo.exe |
| Perform LDAP operations against the directory such as connect, bind, search, modify, add, and delete | Ldp.exe |
| Manage computer accounts, domains, and trust relationships | Netdom.exe |
| Perform database maintenance on the AD DS store, configure AD LDS ports, and view AD LDS instances | Ntdsutil.exe |
| Troubleshoot and diagnose replication problems between domain controllers | Repadmin.exe |

### Directory Services Tools

| Description | Tool |
|---|---|
| Add specific types of objects, such as users, groups, and computers, to the directory | Dsadd.exe |
| Perform maintenance of the AD DS store, configure AD LDS communication ports, and view AD LDS instances | Dsdbutil.exe |
| View the selected properties of a specific object, such as a user or computer, in the directory | Dsget.exe |
| Manage application partitions and operations master roles, and remove metadata from abandoned instances | Dsmgmt.exe |
| Modify an existing object of a specific type, such as a user or computer, in the directory | Dsmod.exe |
| Move an object to a new location within a domain or rename an existing object in the directory | Dsmove.exe |
| Query the directory for a specific object type according to specified criteria | Dsquery.exe |
| Delete an object of a specific type or any general object from the directory | Dsrm.exe |

## Networking and Other Tools

| Description | Tool |
|---|---|
| Repair domain name dependencies in Group Policy objects and links after a domain rename operation | GPfixup.exe |
| Configure a client to use a Kerberos V5 realm instead of an AD DS domain | Ksetup.exe |
| Configure a non-Windows Kerberos service as a security principal in AD DS | Ktpass.exe |
| Perform troubleshooting tasks such as querying replication status and verifying trust relationships | Nltest.exe |
| View information on name servers to diagnose DNS infrastructure problems | Nslookup.exe |
| View settings, manage configuration, and diagnose problems with Windows Time | W32tm.exe |

## Group Policy and Local Policy

Group Policy can be used to configure computer and user settings on networks based on the Active Directory Domain Services AD DS. For Group Policy to work your network must be based on AD DS, and that the computers you want to manage must be joined to the domain. You must also have the relevant permissions to create and edit the policy objects. Although you can also choose to configure Group Policy settings locally, you should avoid doing that since domain-based Group Policy can centralize management while localized policy cannot.

You may manage all aspects of Group Policy via the Group Policy Management Console GPMC, assuming you have joined a domain. From the interface you can see a list of Group Policy objects GPOs which contain the various policy settings. Do note that GPMC is NOT installed by default so you must add it yourself.

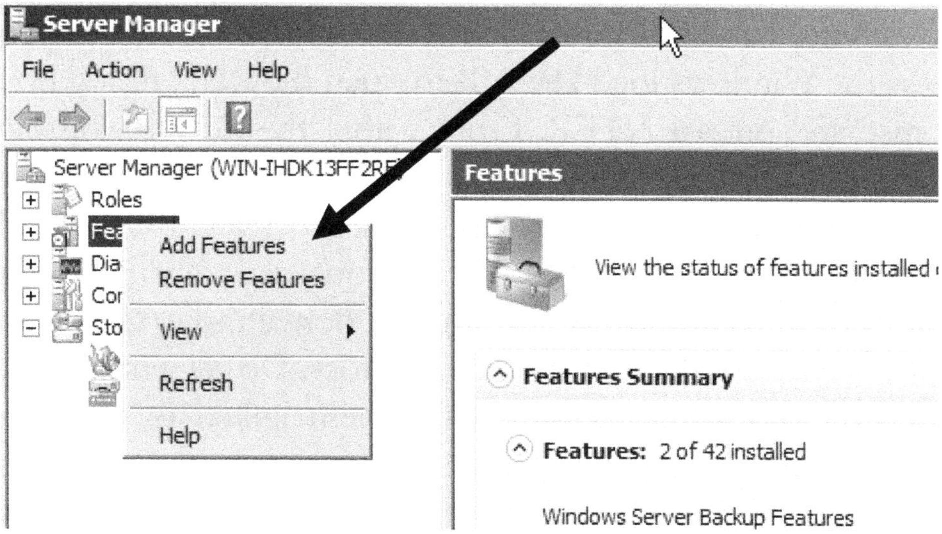
Server Manager
File
Action
View
Help
Server Manager (WIN-IHDK13FF2R
Roles
Fea
Dia
Cor
Sto
Add Features
Remove Features
View
Refresh
Help
Features
View the status of features installed
Features Summary
Features: 2 of 42 installed
Windows Server Backup Features

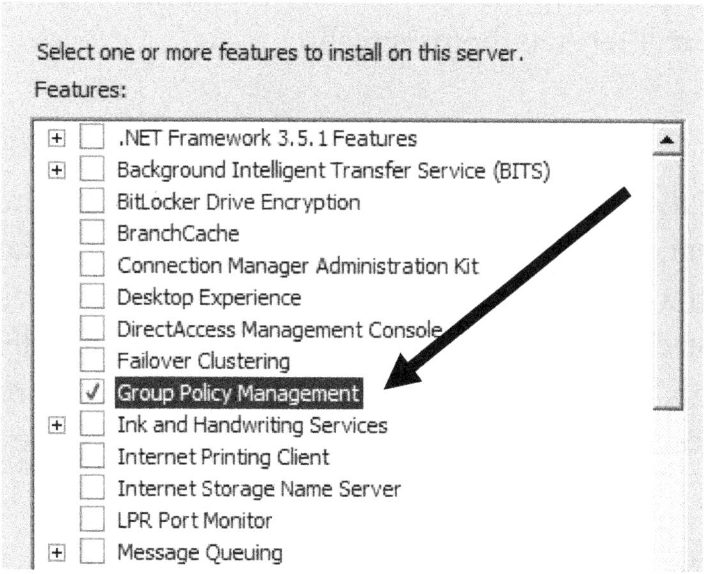
Select one or more features to install on this server.
Features:
.NET Framework 3.5.1 Features
Background Intelligent Transfer Service (BITS)
BitLocker Drive Encryption
BranchCache
Connection Manager Administration Kit
Desktop Experience
DirectAccess Management Console
Failover Clustering
Group Policy Management
Ink and Handwriting Services
Internet Printing Client
Internet Storage Name Server
LPR Port Monitor
Message Queuing

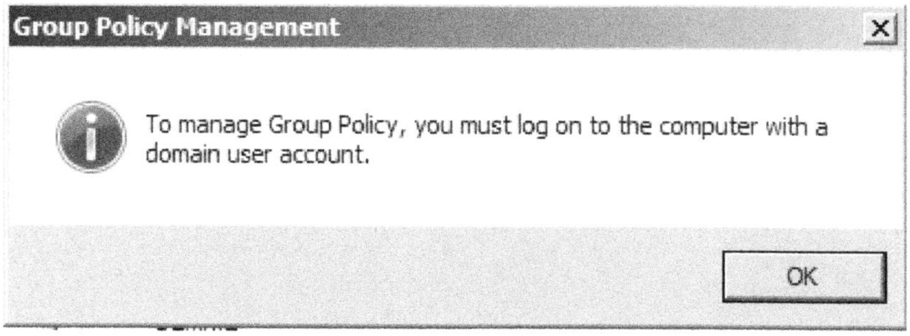
Group Policy Management
To manage Group Policy, you must log on to the computer with a domain user account.
OK

Assuming your computer has been connected to a domain, you may open the GPMC by press the Windows logo key + R to open the RUN dialog box, then enter gpmc.msc and press ENTER. From within the GPMC console tree you can do a lot of things. For example, you can right-click Group Policy Objects in the forest and domain in which you want to create a GPO and then click New to create a new object. You can also add a domain/forest/site here. HOWEVER, adding a domain/site/forest to GPMC does not actually create them in Active Directory. Do remember that GPOs have no impact unless you actually have them linked to a site, a domain, or an OU. At the time you link a GPO to a container, the GPO's settings will be applied to the computers and users in that particular container. Also don't forget about the concept of inheritance. When you link policies to a container, the child containers will receive them as well.

Within the Computer Configuration and User Configuration folders of the GPMC there are two subfolders, which are Policies and Preferences. The former contains policy settings that Group Policy enforces, while Preferences contains preference settings that can be used to change registry setting, file, folder, and the like... Through preference settings you may configure applications and other Windows features that are not Group Policy compatible.

The local policy editor, on the other hand, may be invoked through gpedit.msc.

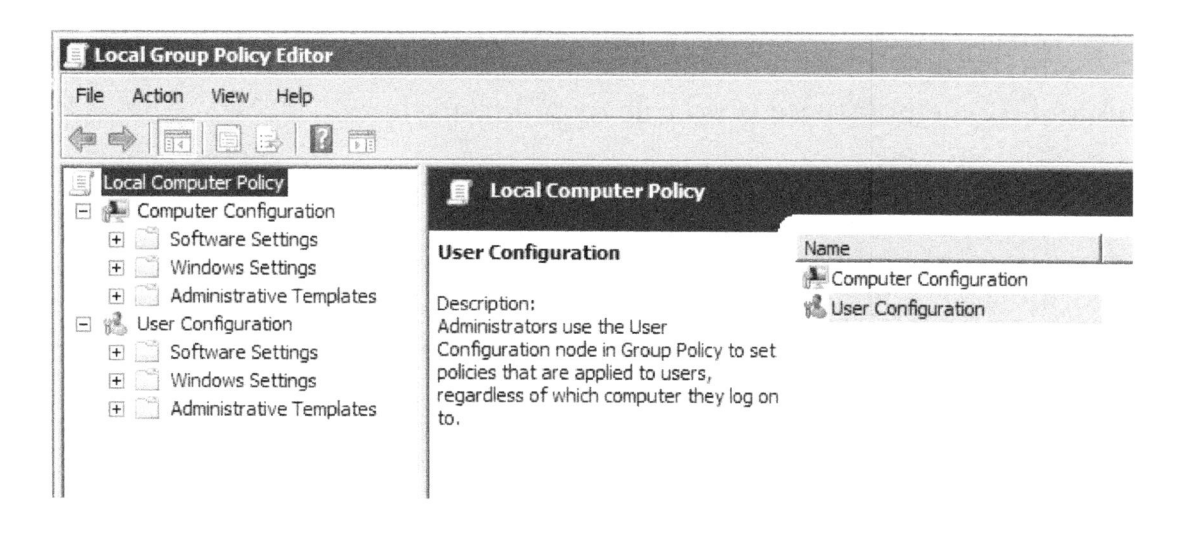

## Software Restrictions

Software restriction policies can be found within the Local Security Policy Editor. Check out the left pane and you will see it there.

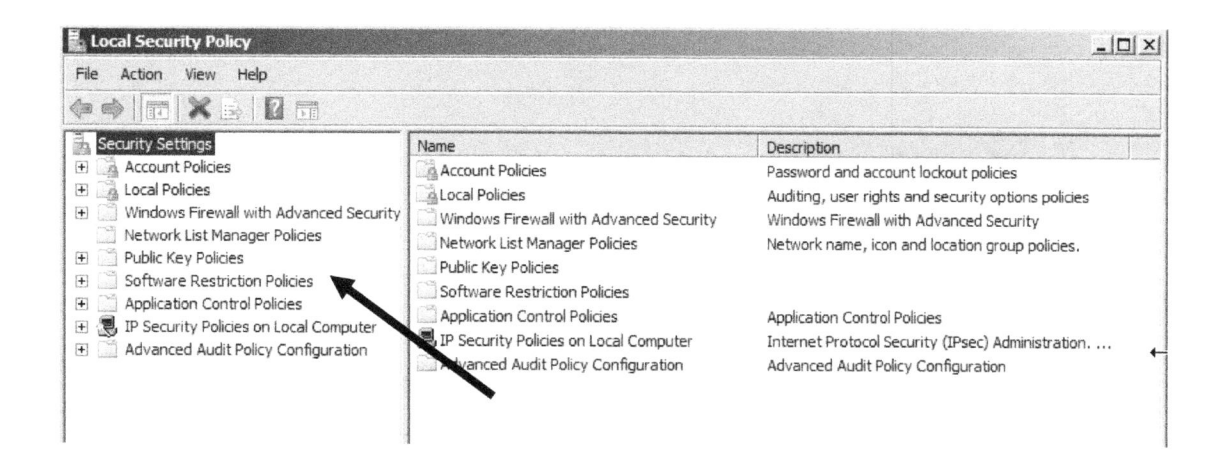

A rule can be Unrestricted or Disallowed. You may have a software restriction policy applied to allow only this list of trusted applications, OR specifically disallow those undesired applications or file types that should be prohibited. By default there is no rule or policy in there.

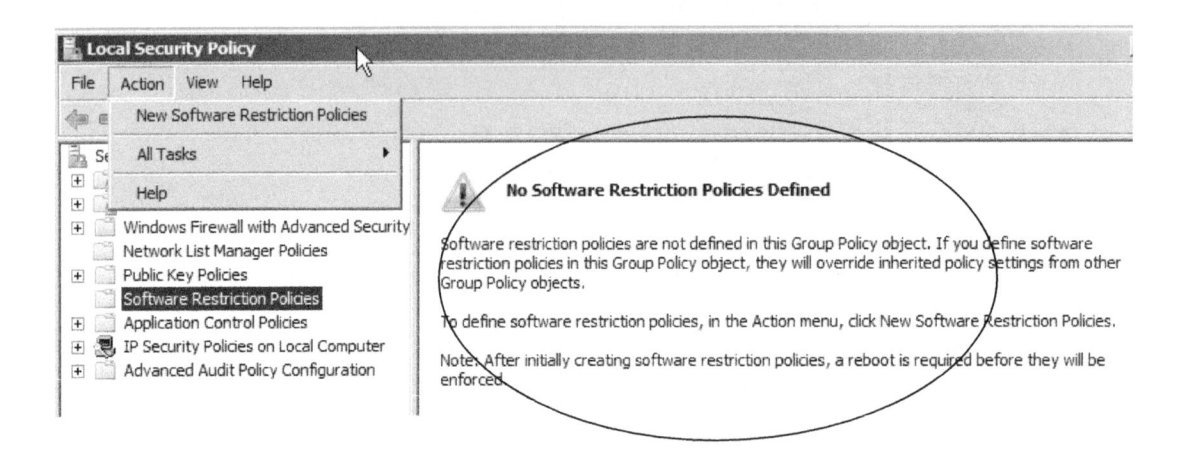

Basic User is kind of a in-between default rule that allows users to execute applications that don't really require administrative privileges. With this rule in place, if you want to allow users to run applications with administrative privileges then you must have a specific rule created.

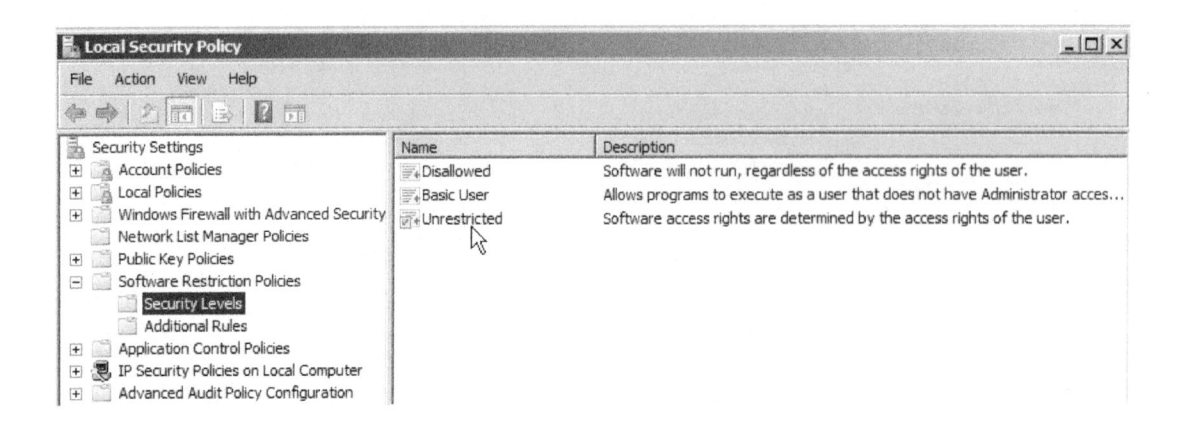

Software Restriction Policies rely on four different types of rule to identify software, which are Hash, Certificate, Path and Zone (Internet zone, as specified in Internet Explorer - in fact this rule applies primarily to Windows Installer packages which may be downloaded through the Internet explorer.). Do realize that these policies will not prevent restricted processes that run under the name of the System account. Different rules do have different drawbacks. Hash rule are specific to files so if you need to hash many files you will have to work on each file one by one. Path Rules cannot be used on folders and files that can change location. Certificate rules are vendor specific so flexibility is lacking when you have different programs from the same vendor. You do want to know that it is possible for rules to have conflicts. The most specific rules take precedence. Remember this order:

1. Hash rules are the most specific!
2. Certificate rules
3. Path rules
4. Zone rules
5. Default rules are the least specific!

The Enforcement Properties policy can be used to specify whether to apply default rules to all files, including libraries or all files excluding libraries. Libraries mean DLLs. Some DLLs can be dangerous!

**AppLocker**

Applocker (from within the Local Security Policy Editor) can be used to configure Application Control Policies so you may choose to block the execution of a software as you see fit. You can have AppLocker rules associated with a specific user or group within an organization. No rules are in place by default. Default rules, if any, should NOT be used for production purpose. You should use the default rules as a template when creating your very own rules only. You also want to know that unlike Software Restriction Policies, an AppLocker rule collection would only function as an allowed list of files, which means only those files that are listed would be allowed to run.

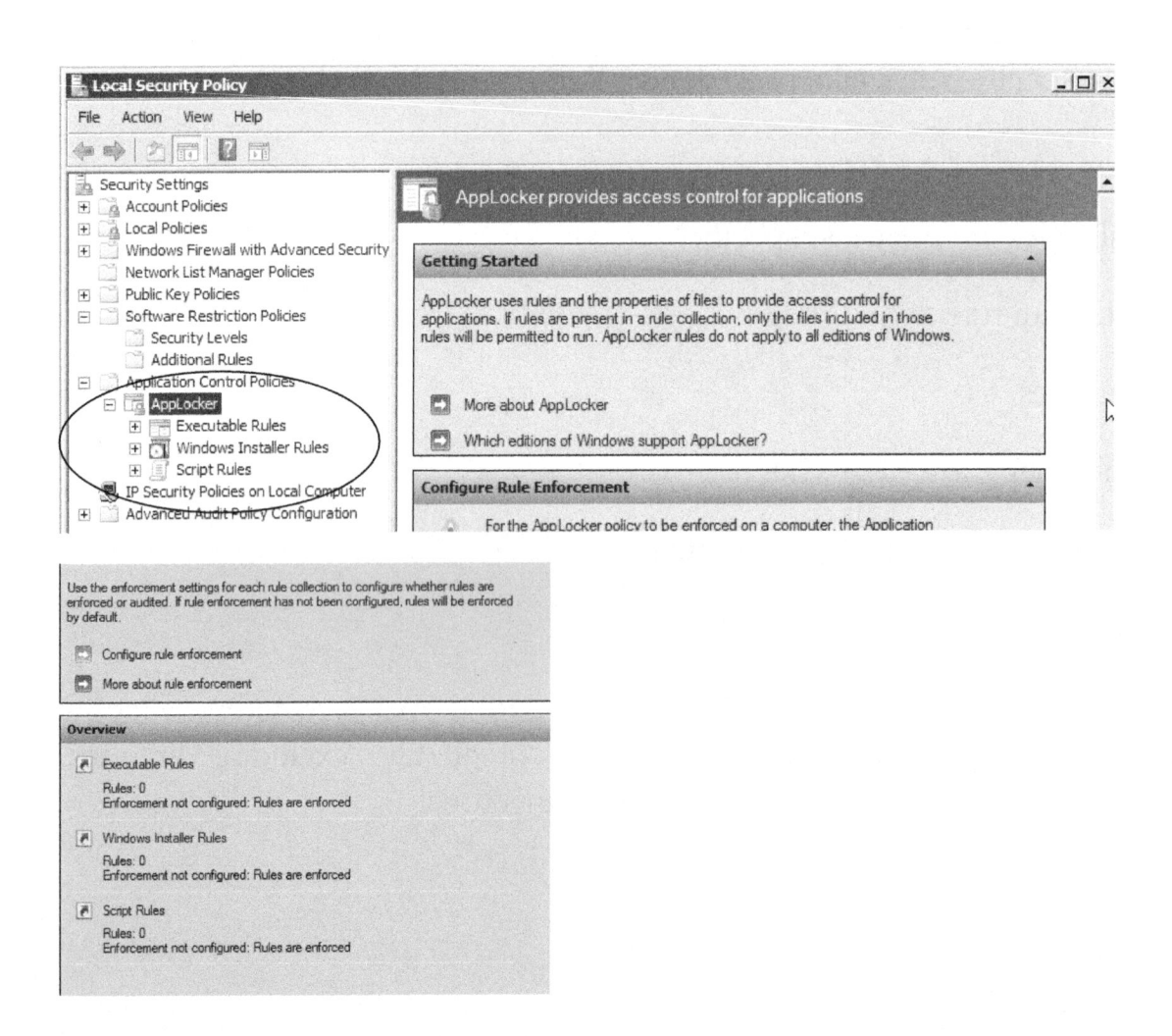

DLL rule collection covers .dll and also .ocx files. The possible defaults are Allows members of the local Administrators group to run all DLLs; Allow all users to run DLLs in the Windows folder; and Allow all users to run DLLs in the Program Files folder. DLL rules may affect system performance! Executable rules cover files with only .exe and .com. The defaults are:

- Allow members of the local Administrators group access to run all executable files
- Allow all users to run executable files in the Windows folder
- Allow all users to run executable files in the Program Files folder

Windows Installer rules cover .msi and .msp files. Script rules cover all these:

- .ps1
- .bat
- .cmd
- .vbs
- .js

AppLocker has a feature to export and import AppLocker policies as an XML file so you may test and modify the policy outside your production environment. After exporting the policy to an XML file, you can import it onto a reference computer for further editing.

## Running a program as an administrator

User Account Control UAC is a feature that can limit privileges of users by default. For the command line to be run as an administrator, right click the icon for the command prompt and choose Run as administrator.

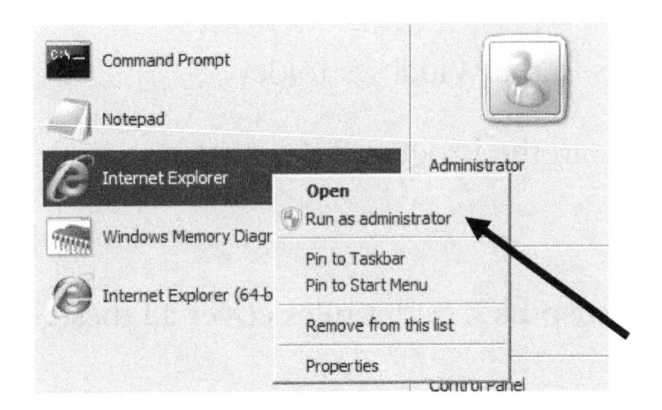

The Run this program as an administrator option may not always be available. When you don't see this option, it could be that:

- the application is blocked from running elevated
- the application does not require administrative credentials to run
- you are not logged on as administrator

## Internet Explorer 8

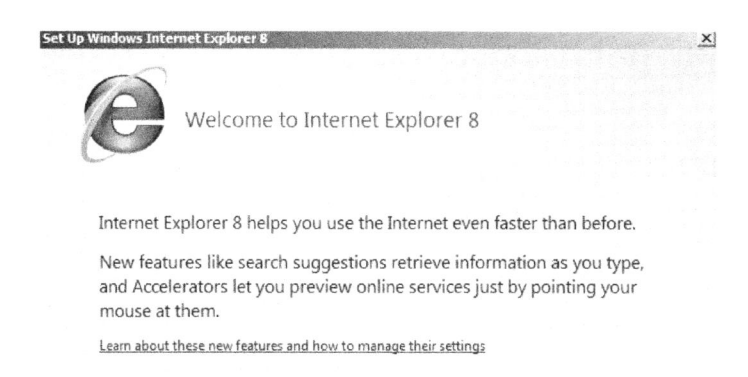

Windows Server 2008 R2 uses IE8 by default. You want to know the different security zones. By default, the level of security set for the Internet zone is applied to all websites, that security level is set to Medium High. The level set for the Local intranet zone is applied to websites and content stored on the corporate network, with security level set to Medium. Level of security set for Trusted sites is applied to sites that have been specifically indicated to be those that you trust. Security level is Medium. The level of security set for Restricted sites is applied to all those sites that may potentially damage your computer. Scripting and active content are not allowed and the security level is set to High. This canNOT be changed.

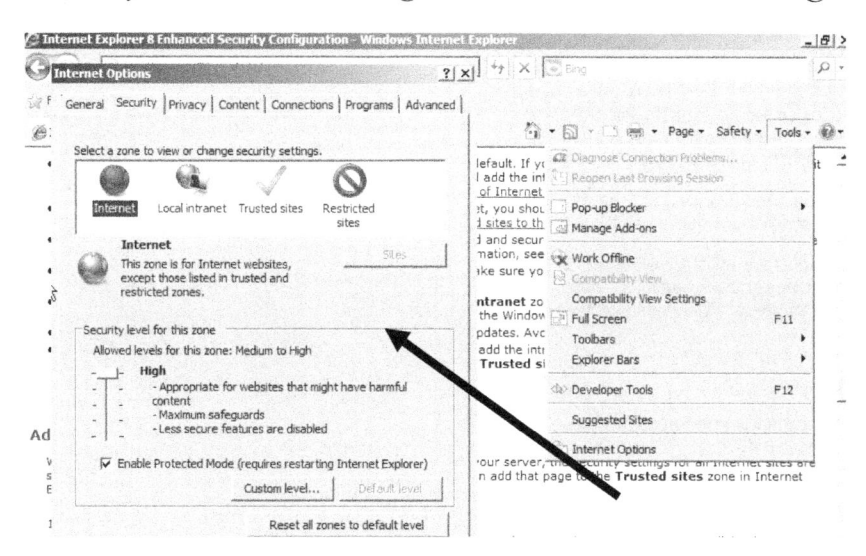

InPrivate Browsing can prevent IE from storing data about the browsing session. This is a security feature.

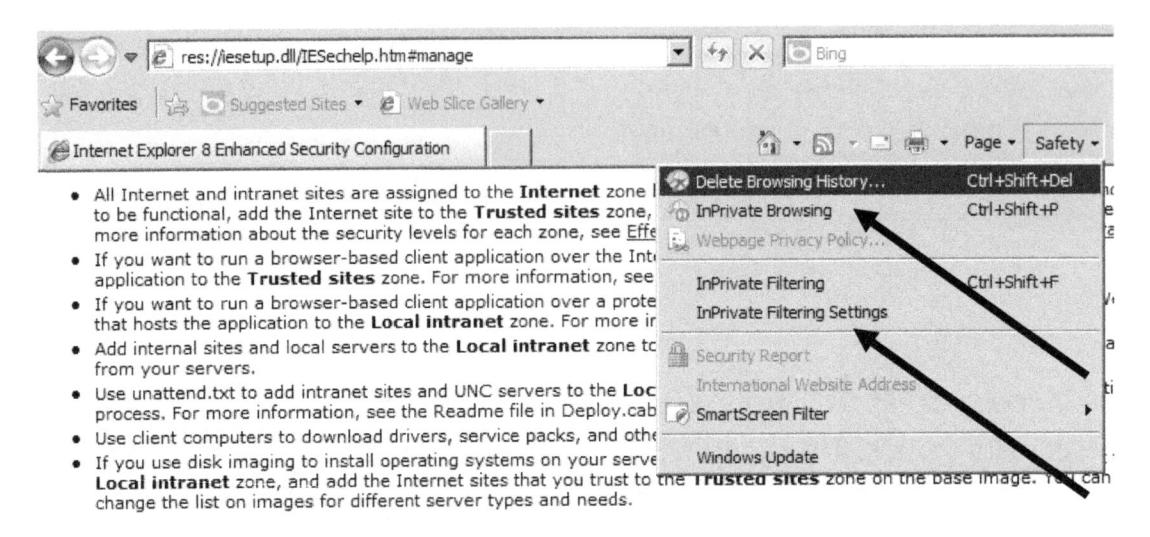

InPrivate Filtering analyzes web content on webpages and sees if the same content is being used on a number of websites. You will be given the option to allow or block that content. The default is to analyze the websites and the content providers they use without automatically blocking them.

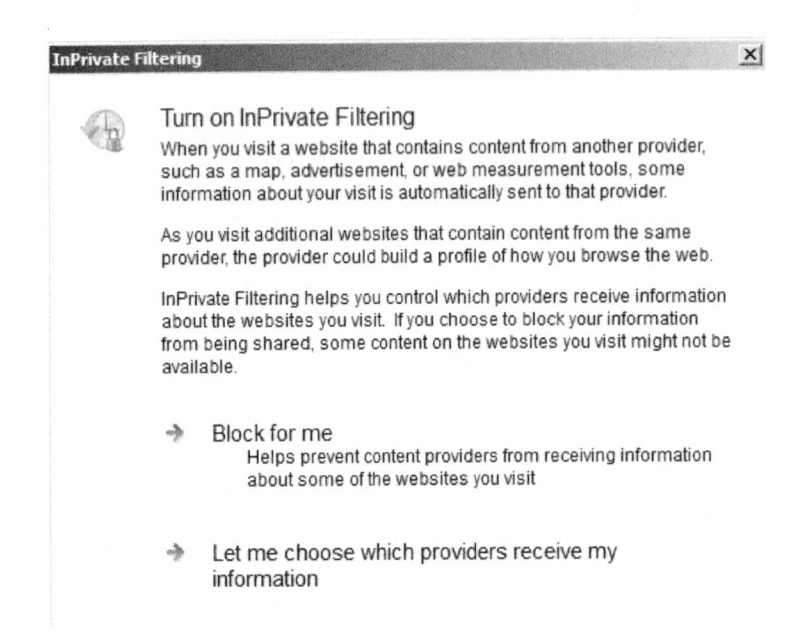

## Device Manager and Device Installation Settings

Windows 2008 R2 supports most new hardware so there is usually no need to use third party drivers. In case you do - if you install a Plug and Play device that has a driver which is not digitally signed, 2008 R2 will not load the unsigned driver. You may disable the signature requirement for the current boot process by starting the computer and press F8, then choose Advanced Boot Options -> Disable Driver Signature Enforcement. Note that signed device drivers is a key security functionality in Windows Server, and that all boot-critical drivers should come with embedded signatures. You may have an unsigned PnP driver installed but administrator credentials will be required. Kernel mode and boot-critical drivers are signed via embedded signing such that every binary in the driver package is signed. Digitally signed PnP drivers, on the other hand, contain a signed .cat file that has a hash of all the files in the corresponding .inf file. In such a setup a signed catalog file will be all that is need to properly install the PnP drivers. Do note that WHQL has a signed driver catalog. However, the need to locate the appropriate catalog file when the operating system loader verifies the driver signature can slow down the booting process.

You use Device Manager to have a graphical overview of all hardware and peripheral devices installed on the computer. Through it you can install and update the drivers for all those hardware devices. The overall functionalities of this MMC console is the same as the earlier version found in 2003 Server. You can update drivers and scan for changes easily.

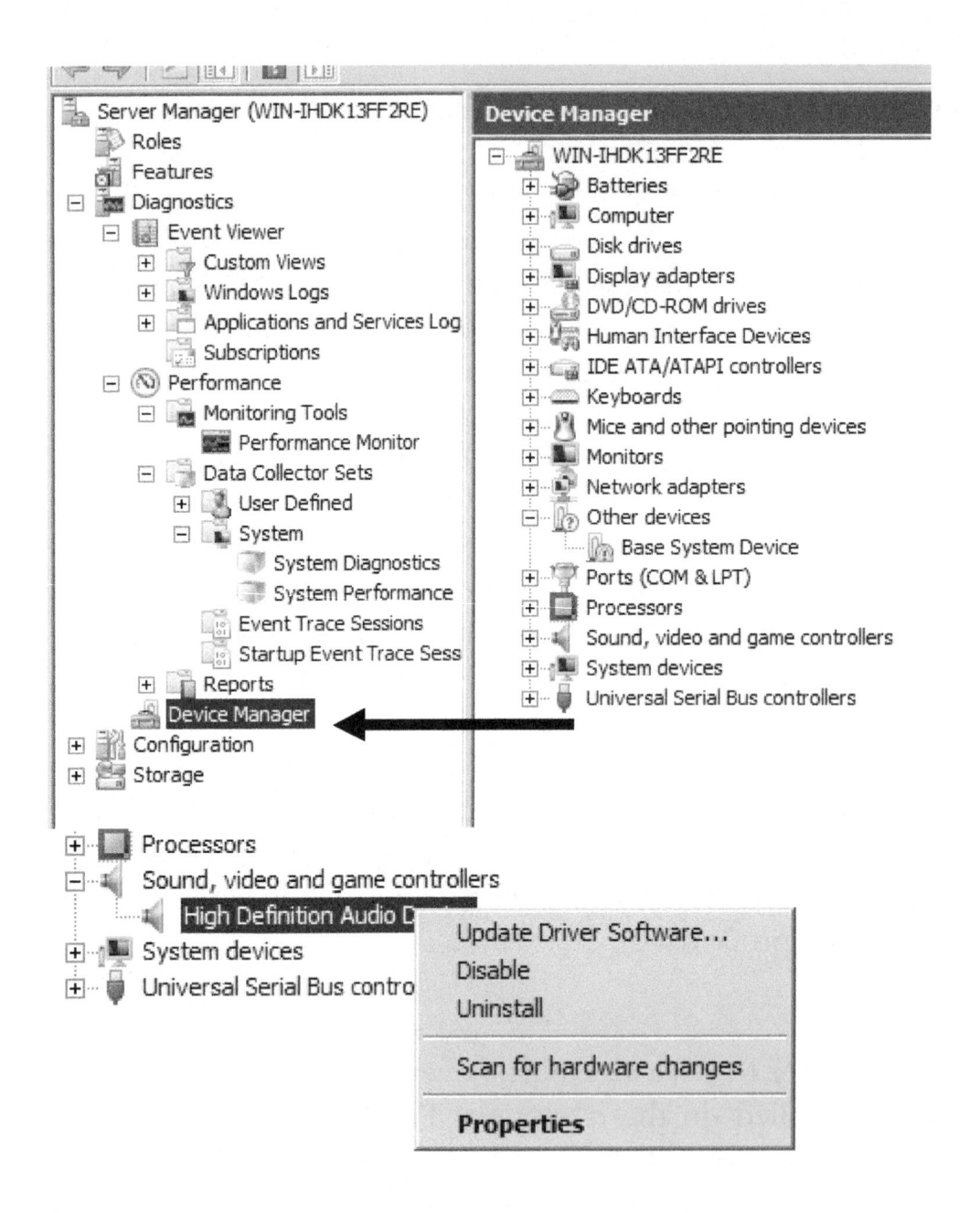

Device Installation Settings deals with automatic driver download. You may allow drivers to be downloaded through Windows Update.

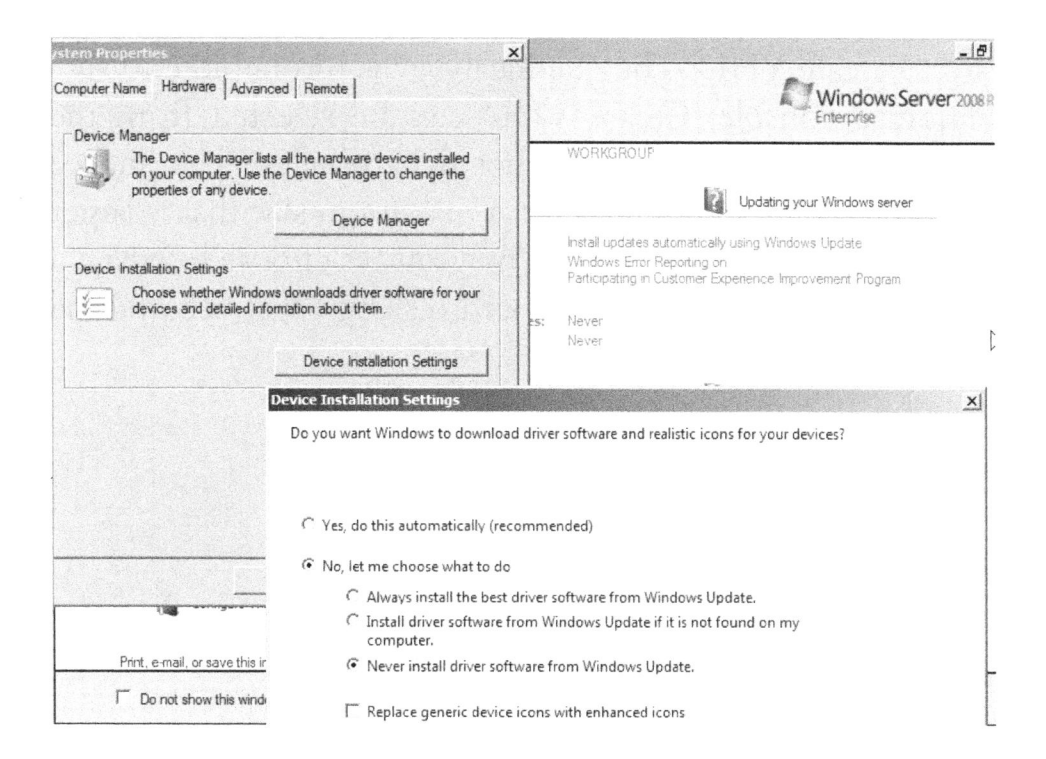

## Configuring VHD

Virtual Hard Disk VHD is a file format for specifying a virtual hard disk to be encapsulated in a single file. This format is being used by Server 2008 Hyper-V, Virtual Server and Virtual PC for virtual disks that are connected to a virtual machine. Think of it as a useful container and also a useful environment for providing a convenient yet isolated test environment. As a means for seamless transition to virtualization, VHD Boot means you boot Windows out of a Virtual Hard Disk file. With this configuration, the VHD file is mounted as a virtual disk but you use it just like using a normal hard disk drive. All the actual data is stored in ONE file, and that you can only run one instance at a time, enjoying almost ALL the power of the computer. This way of running Windows is slightly (only slightly) slower than the normal method of running.

There are two ways to create VHD. The graphical way is through the MMC, using the diskmgmt.msc console. Create VHD can be selected from the Action menu. Virtual hard disk format is either dynamically expanding or fixed. A dynamically expanding VHD can have a maximum size that is larger than the available free space on the drive. You may always choose to create a dynamically expanding VHD, but the virtual hard disk size will become the maximum size the VHD can expand to.

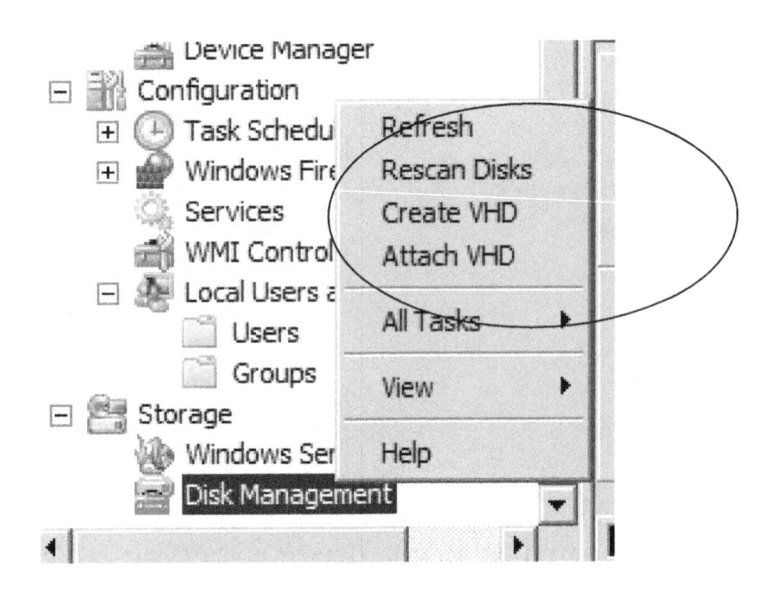

Another way is to use diskpart at the command prompt. First you invoke the diskpart command, then you use the create vdisk command. file= specifies the location and filename of the vhd. maximum= set the size, and type=expandable sets the type to dynamic. Without this the type is fixed.

You can even expand the size of a VHD through diskpart. First make sure that the VHD is detached (you can do this through the MMC easily). Then select it via the select vdisk file= command then type expand vdisk maximum= for specifying the new size. The size unit is in MB. Below shows a series of diskpart commands for attaching (mounting), partitioning, formatting and assigning a drive letter to a VHD.

select vdisk file=c:\myvhd.vhd

attach vdisk

create partition primary

format fs=ntfs label="MyVHD"

assign letter=t


To detach (unmount) the VHD, do these:

select vdisk file=c:\myvhd.vhd

detach vdisk


## Parent and Child VHD

We call this a differencing configuration, which is useful when you have an image serving as a parent VHD that you prefer NOT to modify. Simply put, all modifications to the image are made only to a separate child VHD. In fact the differencing VHD often starts out very small in size, as it only contains the modified disk blocks of the associated parent VHD. The parent VHD is kept as read-only. To create a differencing VHD, you need to use the parent option with the create vdisk command. For example, create vdisk file="c:\thischild.vhd" parent="c:\father.vhd". By configuring parent-child relationships you can form a hierarchy of VHD types, thus increasing manageability and reduce the amount of disk space required since a parent can have many children, and children can have children too. However, when there are too many children the whole thing can become very difficult to manage and can also lead to performance problems. And remember, if you lose the parent VHD then you lose everything.

## Command Line Management Utilities

Windows PowerShell is a command-line shell and scripting language for system administration. It runs on top of the .NET Framework. NetShell is also a command line tool - with it you can remotely administer and configure critical network services. It has an interface which is highly scriptable. Task Scheduler is a tool that can be used to execute tasks at predetermined schedules. Windows Resource Protection WRP is a security feature that can prevent the replacement of essential Windows system files, folders, and registry keys. Applications will not be able to overwrite these resources.

You can use takeown at the command line to reassign ownership of a file. You will need to run it with administrator privileges. You may also use icacls to obtain the control rights to a file. You may use the sc command and its subcommands to manage services via the command prompt. You use sc config to configure service startup and login accounts. You use sc pause to pause a service, or sc continue to resume a paused service. You use sc qc to show the configuration of a particular service, or sc query to examine information on a specified service, driver, type of service, or type of driver.

**Questions:**

1. You may manage all aspects of Group Policy via which interface?

2. Software restriction policies can be found within which interface?

3. What are the primary functions of the Active Directory Certificate Services?

4. What are the primary functions of the Active Directory Domain Services?

5. What are the primary functions of the Active Directory Federation Services?

6. What are the primary functions of the Active Directory Lightweight Directory Services?

7. Software Restriction Policies rely on four different types of rule to identify software, which are:

8. Applocker can be used to configure:

9. DLL rule collection covers what files?

10. What is UAC for?

11. Windows Server 2008 R2 uses which IE version by default?

12. What is InPrivate Browsing?

13. Device Installation Settings deals with:

14. What is the graphical way to create a VHD?

15. Describe Windows PowerShell.

16. Describe WRP.

17. What would you want to configure VHD parent-child relationships?

## **Answers:**

1. *You may manage all aspects of Group Policy via the Group Policy Management Console GPMC, assuming you have joined a domain.*

2. *Software restriction policies can be found within the Local Security Policy Editor.*

3. *Active Directory Certificate Services allows you to create, distribute, and manage customized public key certificates.*

4. *Active Directory Domain Services are responsible for storing directory data and managing communication between users and domains plus administering user logon processes.*

5. *Active Directory Federation Services provides Web single-sign-on for authenticating web user to multiple Web applications.*

6. *Active Directory Lightweight Directory Services provides support for directory-enabled applications.*

7. *Software Restriction Policies rely on four different types of rule to identify software, which are Hash, Certificate, Path and Zone.*

8. *Applocker can be used to configure Application Control Policies so you may choose to block the execution of a software as you see fit.*

9. *DLL rule collection covers .dll and also .ocx files.*

10. *User Account Control UAC is a feature that can limit privileges of users by default.*

11. *Windows Server 2008 R2 uses IE8 by default.*

12. *InPrivate Browsing can prevent IE from storing data about the browsing session. This is a security feature.*

13. *Device Installation Settings deals with automatic driver download.*

14. *There are two ways to create VHD. The graphical way is through the MMC, using the diskmgmt.msc console.*

15. *Windows PowerShell is a command-line shell and scripting language for system administration. It runs on top of the .NET Framework.*

16. *Windows Resource Protection WRP is a security feature that can prevent the replacement of essential Windows system files, folders, and registry keys. Applications will not be able to overwrite these resources.*

17. *By configuring parent-child relationships you can form a hierarchy of VHD types, thus increasing manageability and reduce the amount of disk space required since a parent can have many children, and children can have children too.*

# Server 2008 R2 Installation and Configuration

## Pre-installation prep works

You need to have a DVD drive. You need to set the BIOS to boot from it. Also, before performing an install/upgrade, these are the MUST -DOs:

- Back up your server if you are going to install onto a working one, including all data and configuration information.
- Disconnect all UPS devices to avoid issues with the port detection process. And disable all virus protection software as they may interfere with the installation process.
- Use the Windows Memory Diagnostic tool to test the RAM module on the computer to avoid potential memory error issues.

In fact there is a tool you can use to check memory even after Windows Server is installed. It is called Windows Memory Diagnostic.

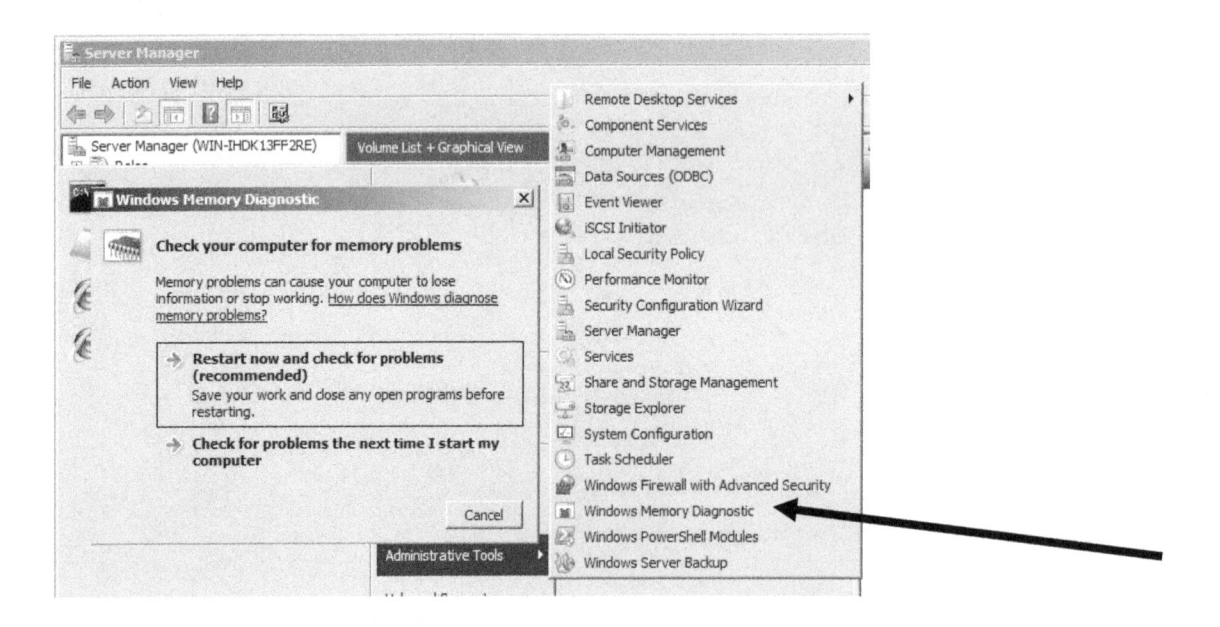

In a domain environment running active directory AD, prior to adding a domain controller running 2008 R2 to an Active Directory forest or upgrade an existing domain controller to 2008 R2, you should first run Adprep.exe from the 2008 R2 media on your existing domain controllers to prepare your domain and forest. To prepare a forest you must log on to the schema master. And you must log on as a member of the Enterprise Admins, Schema Admins, or Domain Admins group. You then copy the contents of the \support\adprep folder from the 2008 R2 installation DVD to the schema master role holder. At the command line, run adprep /forestprep. On the other hand, to prepare a domain you should first log on to the infrastructure master as a member of the Domain Admins group, then copy the contents of the adprep folder to the infrastructure master role holder. Execute the command adprep /domainprep /gpprep.


### Administrator Account

When you set up Windows Server, you need to use a local administrator account that allows you to set up the computer and install the necessary programs. **You have no way to delete this account.** BEWARE: A local administrator is an admin with full rights over the local machine only. A Domain Administrator has admin rights access over the entire domain. The Enterprise Admin is said to have God rights everywhere in the network. Keep in mind, after installation you must set a complex password for this account. The password must be a complex one, with letters, numbers and symbols included. You may also use this command to require password and take the chance to change to a strong password: net user Administrator <password>/passwordreq:yes

MS defines a "strong password" as one which is at least seven characters long and without using user name, real name, company name or complete dictionary word. It should also be one significantly different from previous passwords (if any). You may in fact create passwords that contain characters from the extended ASCII character set, which can increase the number of characters that you may use when creating a password.

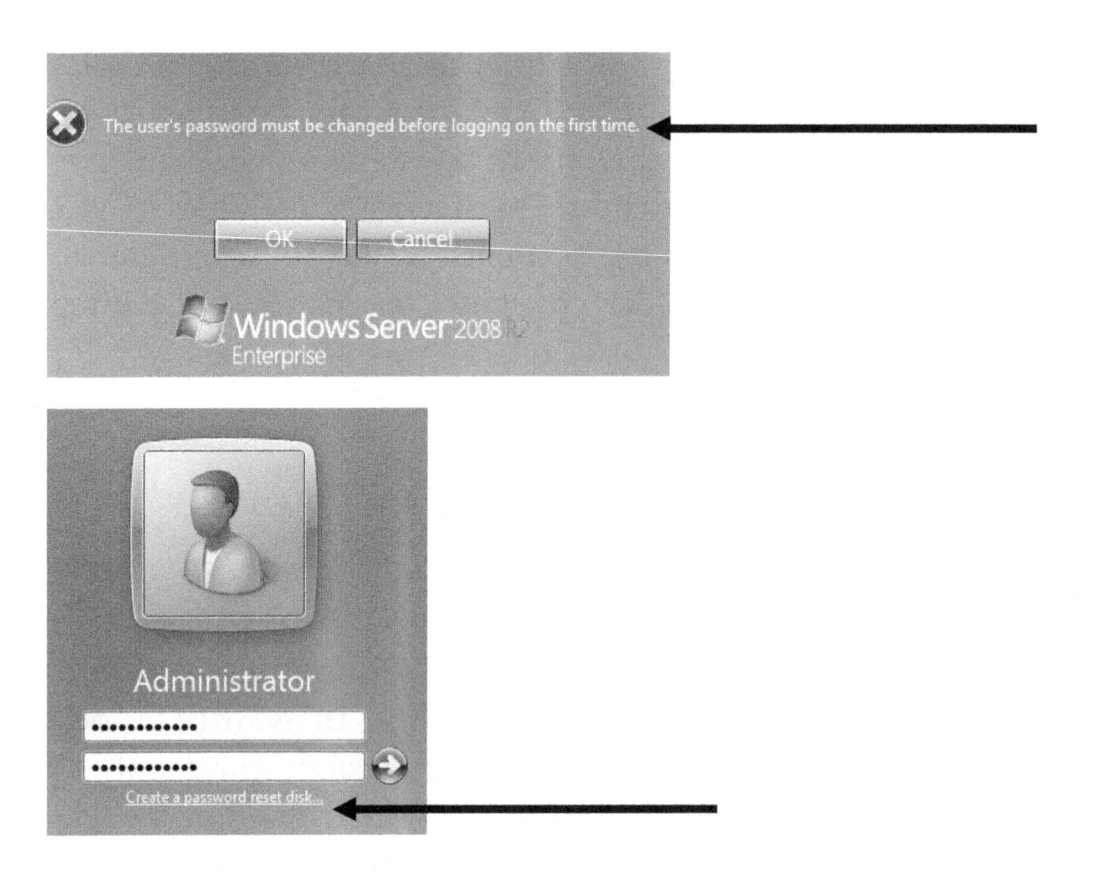

You also have the option to create a password reset disk. Note that a password reset disk can only be used for local computer accounts. You cannot use it for domain accounts. You also cannot change your password and create a password reset disk at the same time. HOWEVER, you are free to change your password any time after creating a password reset disk. Other changes related to the administrator account and other user accounts can be made via the Server Manager:

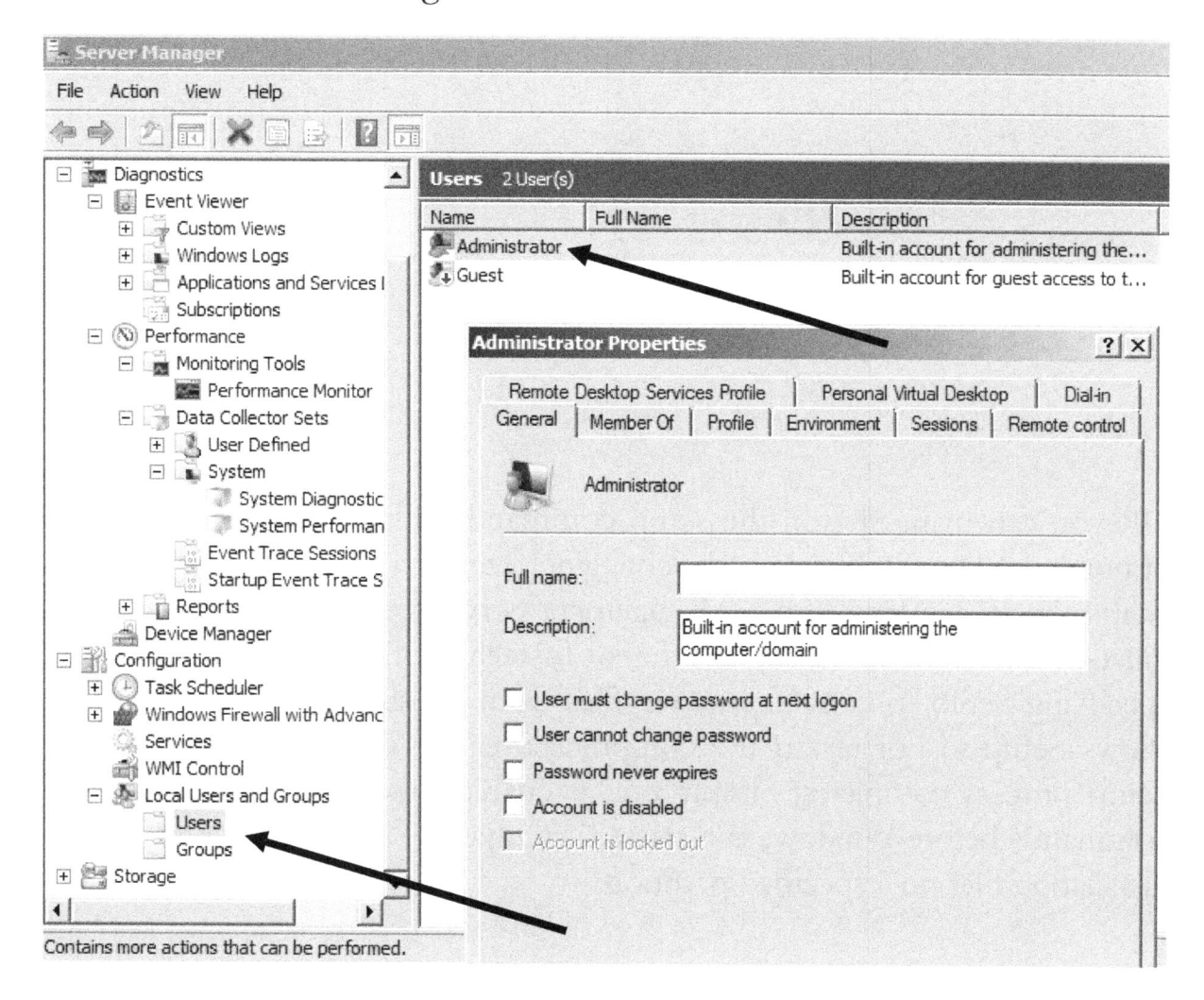

## Manual Installation VS Unattended Installation

When performing a manual installation process, you simply run the Setup program from the DVD media and answer each prompt. You can boot up your machine using the DVD media. **Boot the system via the DVD. Select the language and input method. When you see the setup screen, choose "Install Now".**

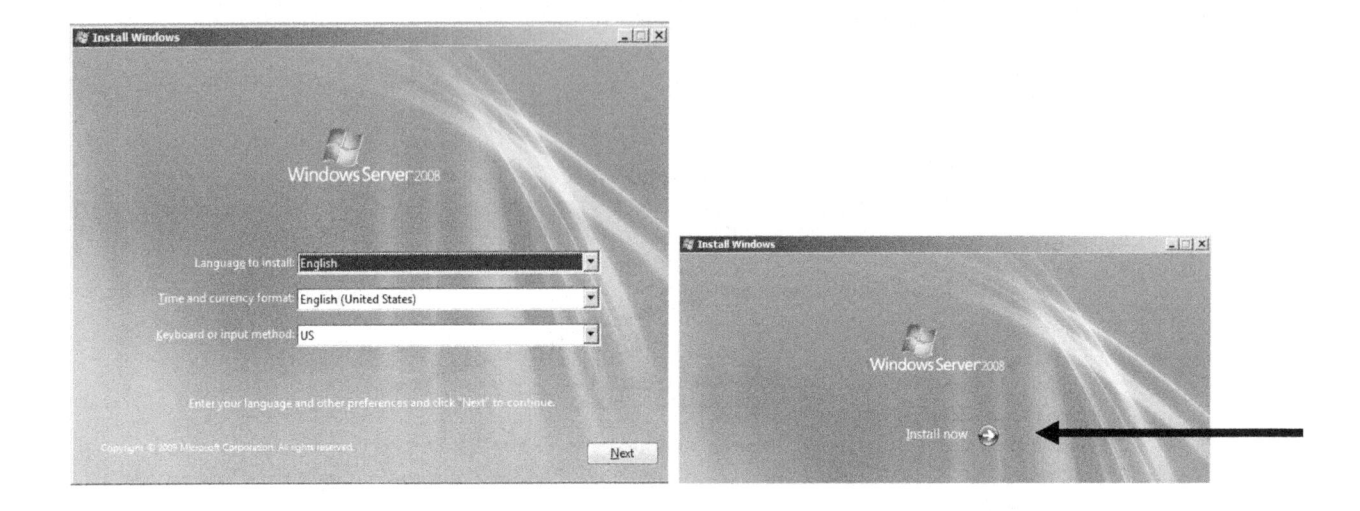

OR you can manually run the setup command. This command has several options. /debug enables kernel debugging over a com port. /emsport can enable or disable Emergency Management Services during Windows Setup. /installfrom: is for specifying a different Install.wim file to be used. /m is for specifying Setup to copy alternative files from another location. /noreboot allows Setup to not restart the computer after the downlevel phase of the Setup process completes. Simply put, it enables one to execute additional commands before Windows is restarted. /tempdrive is for placing temporary installation files on a specified partition.

/unattend is for enabling the unattended setup mode. You may explicitly specify the use of an answer file by invoking the setup.exe command with the /unattend:filename switch. The answer file can be used to configure the Windows installation. By default, it is named Unattend.xml. When the answer file is not specified, Windows Setup can still automatically search for an answer file in several default locations.

You may create an Unattend.xml file via Notepad or the Windows SIM System Image Manager. Keep in mind, answer files are cached to the computer during Setup and that they will persist between reboots. Before delivering the computer, you should delete the cached answer file located in the %WINDIR%\panther directory.

To actually perform unattended setup, one suggested way is to first create the Unattend.xml file via a text editor, then copy it to a local drive or a shared network drive. You then boot your computer to Windows PE. Insert the DVD media containing Windows Server 2008 R2 into your DVD drive. At the command prompt, change to the drive that contains the installation media and type the command setup /unattend: referencing the xml file.

The DVD media includes different installations for you to choose from.

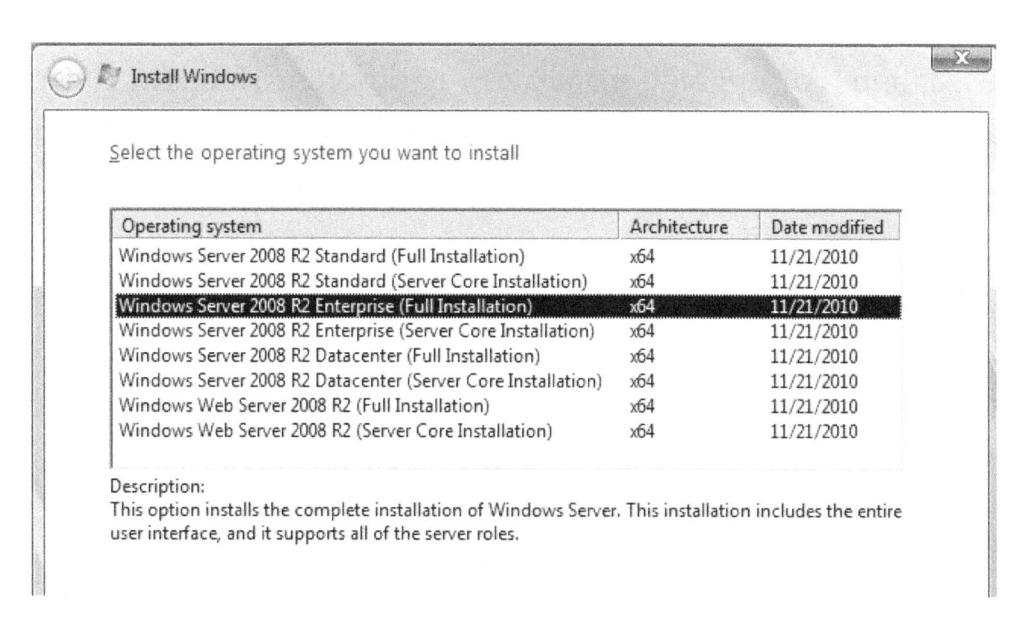

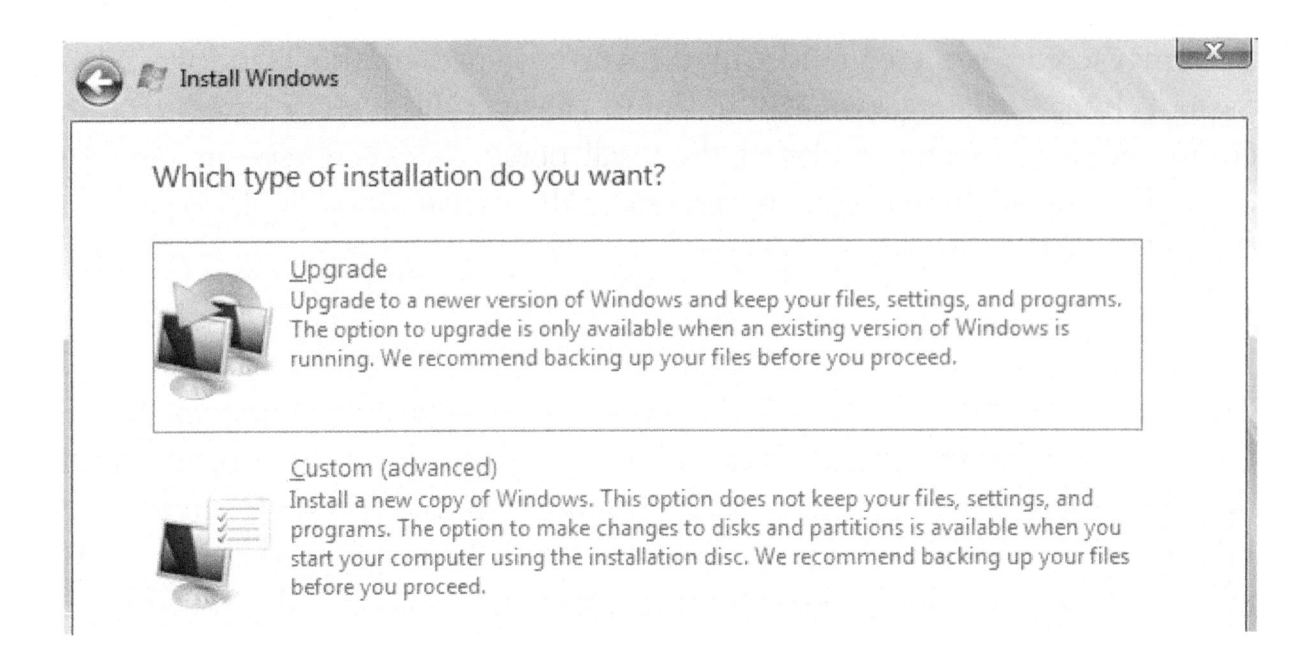

Windows Setup can perform two types of installation, which are clean and upgrade. It is for installation on a single machine. A custom installation is a clean installation that saves previous Windows installation without migrating the settings. The previous Windows installation will no longer to able to boot after a clean installation. An upgrade installation is different as it can retain previous settings and preferences.

## Disk partitioning

If you perform manual installation, at the time setup is proceeding you have the chance to prepare the disk partition:

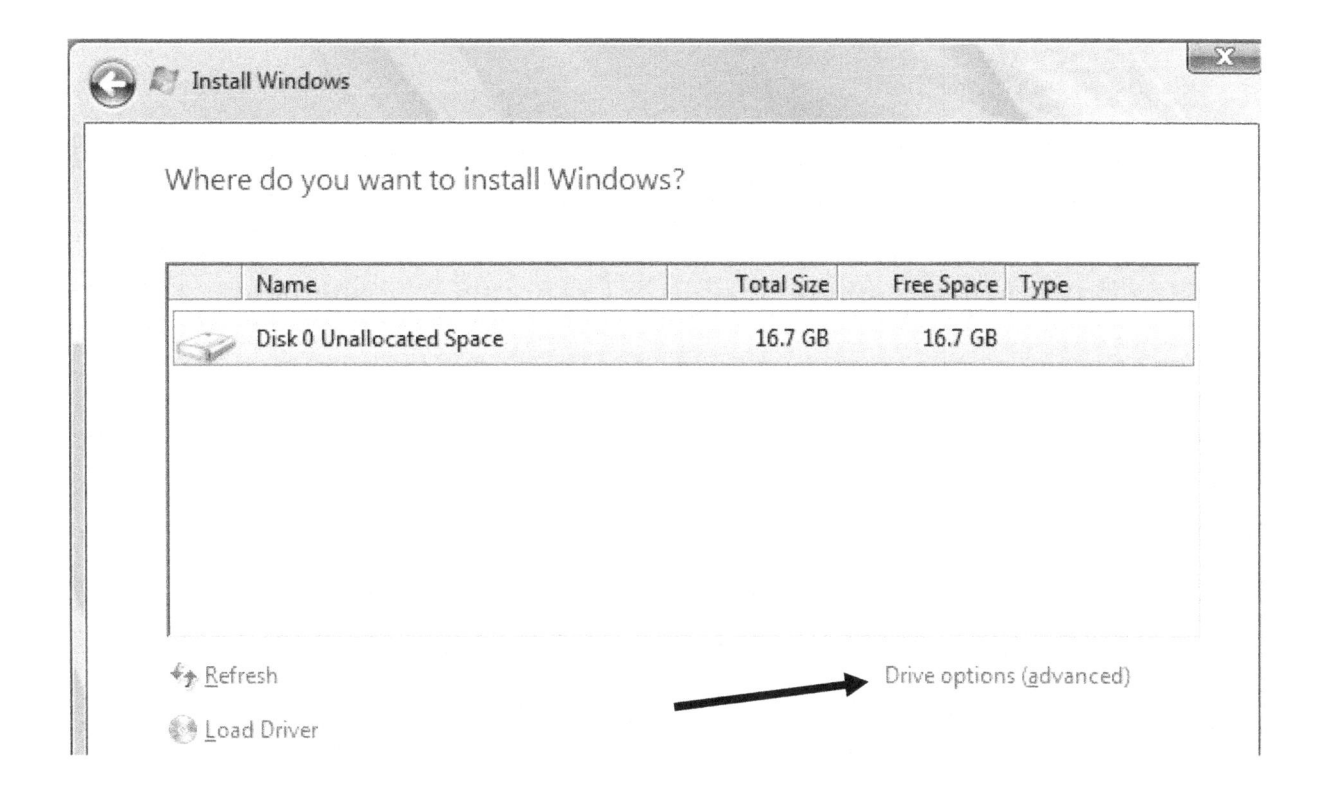

With the traditional BIOS-Based computers you need to format hard drives using an MBR file system. Each disk can have up to four standard partitions and the computer must boot to the active partition. Only one primary partition can be set to active. Also, each partition can have max 2TB of space only.

Windows Server 2008 R2 also supports EFI-based or UEFI-based computer. You can have max 128 primary partitions for storing files and utilities. You need to format the hard disk drive using a GUID partition table GPT file system. With the EFI System Partition each bootable drive must contain an ESP so that the computer can boot to this partition. A Microsoft Reserved Partition MSR is a reserved partition that does not have a partition ID. It cannot store user data but solely for management purpose. Its size is 128 MB.

System partitions can be used to manage and load other partitions, as well as to use recovery tools such as the Windows Recovery Environment Windows RE. Note that system partitions will not show up in the list of available drives but will still be visible in Computer Management.

Each system partition must have at least 100MB of space plus free space for creating shadow copies. A MSR partition must have at least 128 MB of hard drive space. A Windows partition must have at least 15GB of drive space, with 700 MB of freely available space during Windows Setup.

An unformatted disk is first initialized with no partitions on it. Since every disk must contain at least one partition, you need to have one created within a volume via the Disk Management console.

A New Simple Volume is the easiest thing to use as the New Simple Volume Wizard will guide you through the whole process. Diskpart, on the other hand, is a command line tool. You need to deal with commands, not graphical interface. An easy way to enter diskpart is to boot the system via the DVD. When you see the setup screen, do not choose anything but press "Shift-F10" to get into the command line. Enter diskpart so you may start the partitioning utility.

## DISM

The Deployment Image Servicing and Management DISM tool can be used to build and deploy Windows images offline. It is a scriptable command-line utility. Through it you may mount and unmount system images as well as update operating system components. DISM can support Windows 7, Vista with SP1/2, Server 2008/2008 R2 and Windows PE 3.0.

You want to know that DISM is not the right choice for installing packages to a remote computer over a network. For DISM to work, the Windows image must be local. If you specify an answer file as unattend.xml for the image, keep in mind only those settings specified in the offlineServicing configuration pass will be applied. Generally, DISM can only be used to install .cab files, .msu files, and .inf files. It can also be used with some older Windows image files in the .wim format. HOWEVER, Microsoft System Installer system .msi files are not supported - they must be installed online via OCSetup.

OCSetup is a command-line utility you may use for applying updates to an online Windows image. It can used to install .msi files via MSIExec.exe. It can also install and remove Component-Based Servicing CBS packages online by passing packages to DISM. Do remember that in order to make use of OCSetup, the system MSI packages must be staged before they can be installed. Also, the paths to the packages must be specified in an answer file properly. Staging an installer file means placing the file in the location specified by the CustomSetup registry key or %WINSYSDIR%\SysMSI\Stage\. To run OCSetup you must first set the command prompt to run as an administrator.

If you need to install a package that requires a custom installer, you will have to first register the name of the package by editing this registry key: HKEY_LOCAL_MACHINE\SOFTWARE\Microsoft\Windows\Current Version\Setup\OC Setup\Components\

## Windows PE and WDS

Windows PE Preinstallation Environment is a minimal operating system for preparing a computer for Windows installation. It is available as a standalone product to those with proper licensing agreement. It is also an integrated component of Windows Setup and Windows Deployment Services. You use BCDboot to quickly set up a system partition or to repair the boot environment of the system partition. You use BCDEdit to manage BCD stores. You use Bootsect.exe to update the master boot code for hard disk partitions or to restore the boot sector. You use Oscdimg to create an image in the format of .iso for your customized Windows PE. You use Expand.exe to expand and open up the compressed update files. You use Intlcfg.exe to change the language and locale, fonts, and input settings...etc for an installation.

The X drive is a RAM disk. By default it is allocated 32 MB, although you can customize the size via the PEImg.exe utility. Any changes you make to the Windows PE registry will be lost upon reboot unless you make the changes when Windows PE is not online. Also, there is no .NET Framework support.

You may consider using Windows Deployment Services WDS for OS deployment. WDS is actually the updated and redesigned version of Remote Installation Services RIS. Through it you may deploy Windows operating systems over the network. However, a number of things are required. You need to have existing servers acting as the Deployment Server and also the Transport Server. They must join a domain, and must be supported by DHCP and DNS. On the Deployment Server, run the command

ServerManagerCmd -install WDS. On the Transport Server, run ServerManagerCmd -install WDS-Transport.

You need to add at least one boot image and also one install image so you can boot to the Windows Deployment Services server and install an image. Note that the client computer must be capable of performing a PXE boot and must meet the hardware requirements for the operating system of the install image. It also needs at least 512 MB of RAM.

## Initial configuration

After installation is completed, when you start Server 2008 R2 the Initial Configuration Tasks Wizard will automatically come up:

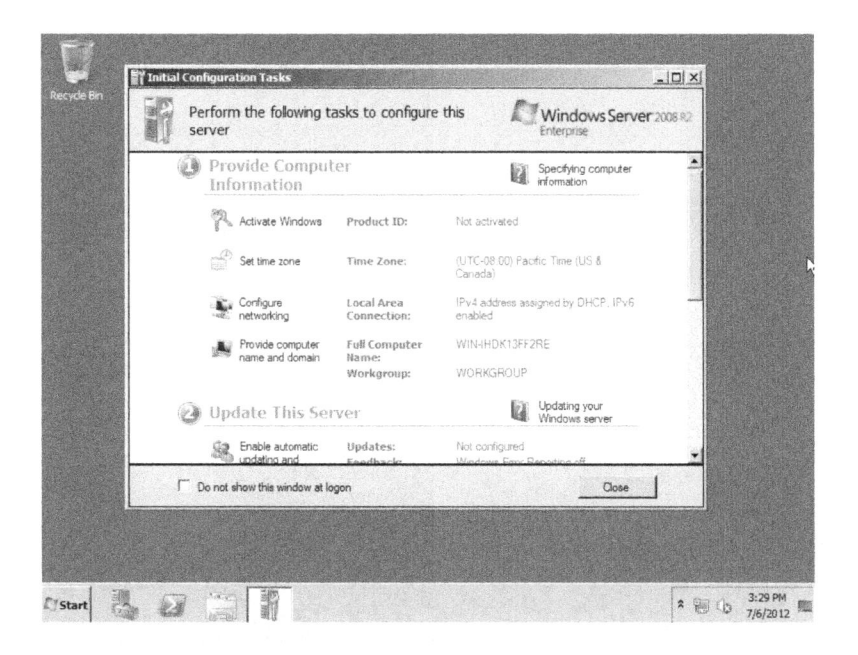

If you want to check the computer name or the workgroup/domain name, use Control Panel instead.

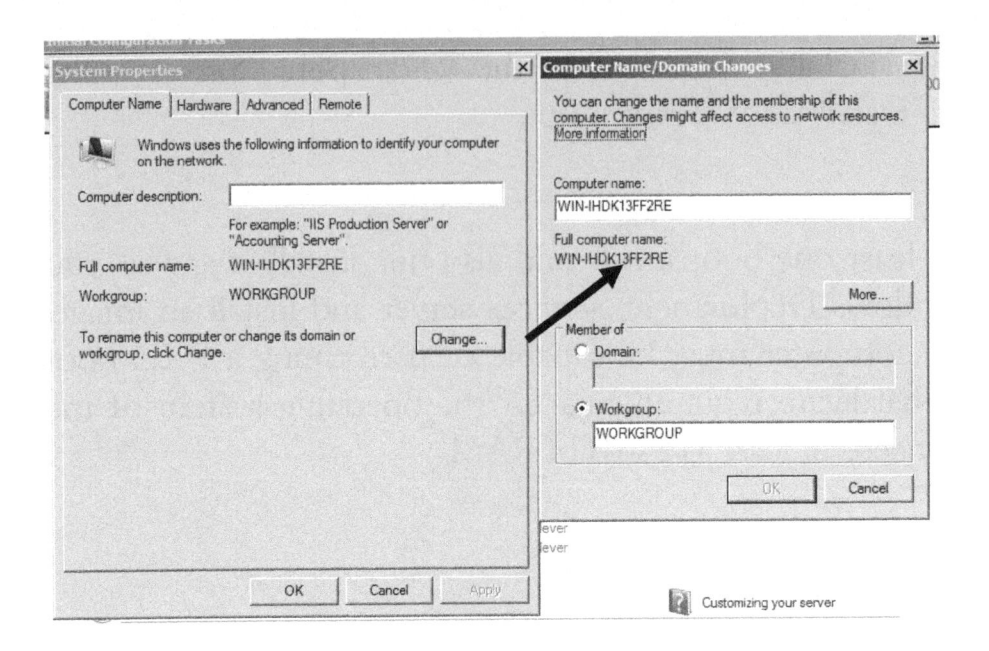

## The Server Migration tool

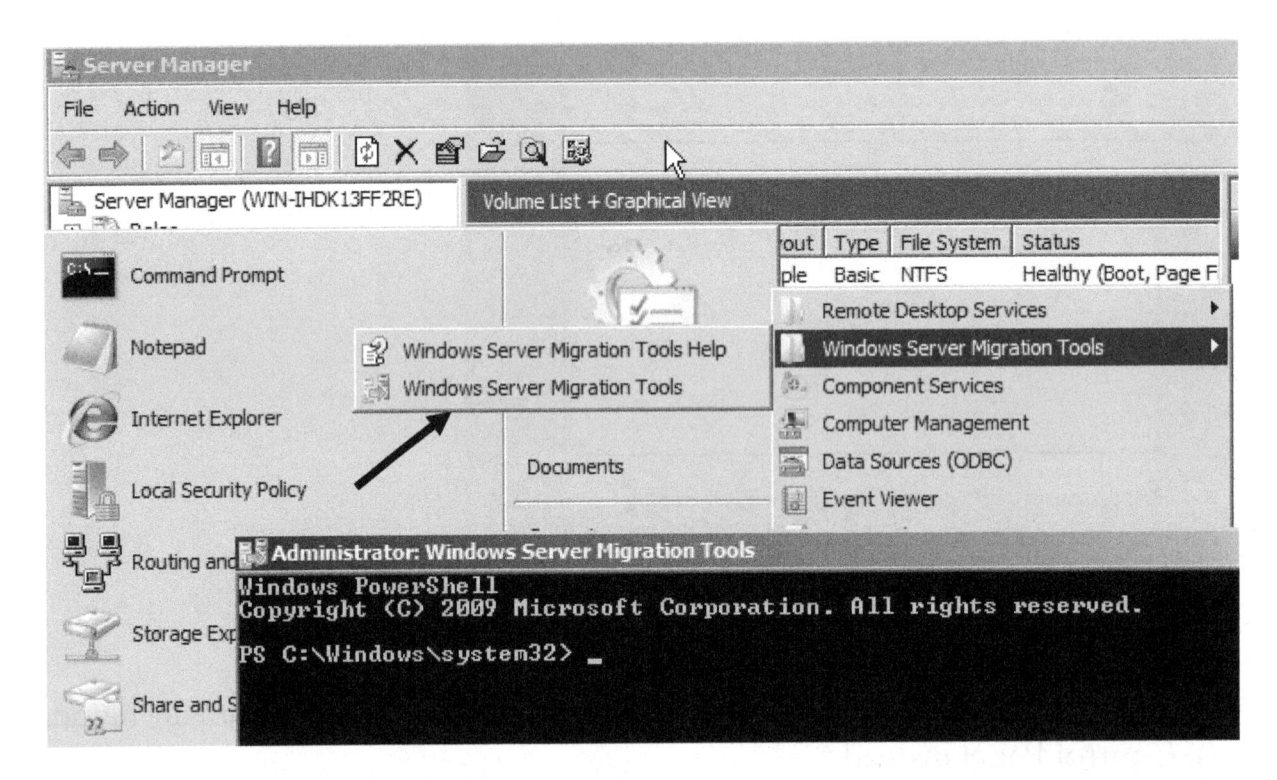

The Windows Server Migration Tools can use the following editions of Windows Server as either the source or the destination:

- Windows Server Foundation
- Windows Server Standard
- Windows Server Enterprise
- Windows Server Datacenter

You can install Windows Server Migration Tools on Windows Server 2008 R2 by using the Server Manager console. You simply need to add a feature from within it. If this is a server core installation, you need to use Powershell, Import-Module ServerManager and then Add-WindowsFeature. You then use smigdeploy.exe to create deployment folders for the source computers. Source OS could be 2003 Server R2 or 2003 Server with SP2 or any version of 2008 Server. Migration between a physical OS and a virtual OS is supported. Migration between OS with different system UI language is not possible though.

## Questions:

1. Prior to adding a domain controller running 2008 R2 to a forest or upgrade an existing domain controller to 2008 R2, you should first run _____ to prepare your domain and forest.

2. Compare the different types of administrator.

3. MS defines a "strong password" as one which is:

4. What are the limitations of password reset disk?

5. The answer file has a default name of:

6. /debug is a setup command option for:

7. /emsport is a setup command option for:

8. Compare a custom installation with an upgrade installation.

9. For DISM to work, the Windows image must be local. True?

10. Windows PE Preinstallation Environment is a minimal operating system for what purpose?

11. Windows PE is an integrated component of Windows Setup and:

12. The Windows Server Migration Tools can use what editions of Windows Server as either source or destination?

13. What is smigdeploy.exe for?


## Answers:

1. *In a domain environment running active directory AD, prior to adding a domain controller running 2008 R2 to an Active Directory forest or upgrade an existing domain controller to 2008 R2, you should first run Adprep.exe from the 2008 R2 media on your existing domain controllers to prepare your domain and forest.*

2. *A local administrator is an admin with full rights over the local machine only. A Domain Administrator has admin rights access over the entire domain. The Enterprise Admin is said to have God rights everywhere in the network.*

3. *MS defines a "strong password" as one which is at least seven characters long and without using user name, real name, company name or complete dictionary word. It should also be one significantly different from previous passwords (if any).*

4. *A password reset disk can only be used for local computer accounts. You cannot use it for domain accounts. You also cannot change your password and create a password reset disk at the same time.*

5. *The answer file can be used to configure the Windows installation. By default, it is named Unattend.xml.*

6. */debug enables kernel debugging over a com port.*

7. */emsport can enable or disable Emergency Management Services during Windows Setup.*

8. *A custom installation is a clean installation that saves previous Windows installation without migrating the settings. The previous Windows installation will no longer to able to boot after a clean installation. An upgrade installation is different as it can retain previous settings and preferences.*

9. *For DISM to work, the Windows image must be local.*

10. *Windows PE Preinstallation Environment is a minimal operating system for preparing a computer for Windows installation. It is available as a standalone product to those with proper licensing agreement.*

11. *It is an integrated component of Windows Setup and Windows Deployment Services.*

12. *Windows Server Foundation, Windows Server Standard, Windows Server Enterprise, Windows Server Datacenter*

13. *You use smigdeploy.exe to create deployment folders for the source computers during a migration.*

# Network Settings, Security and Remote/Mobile Access

## Network Location

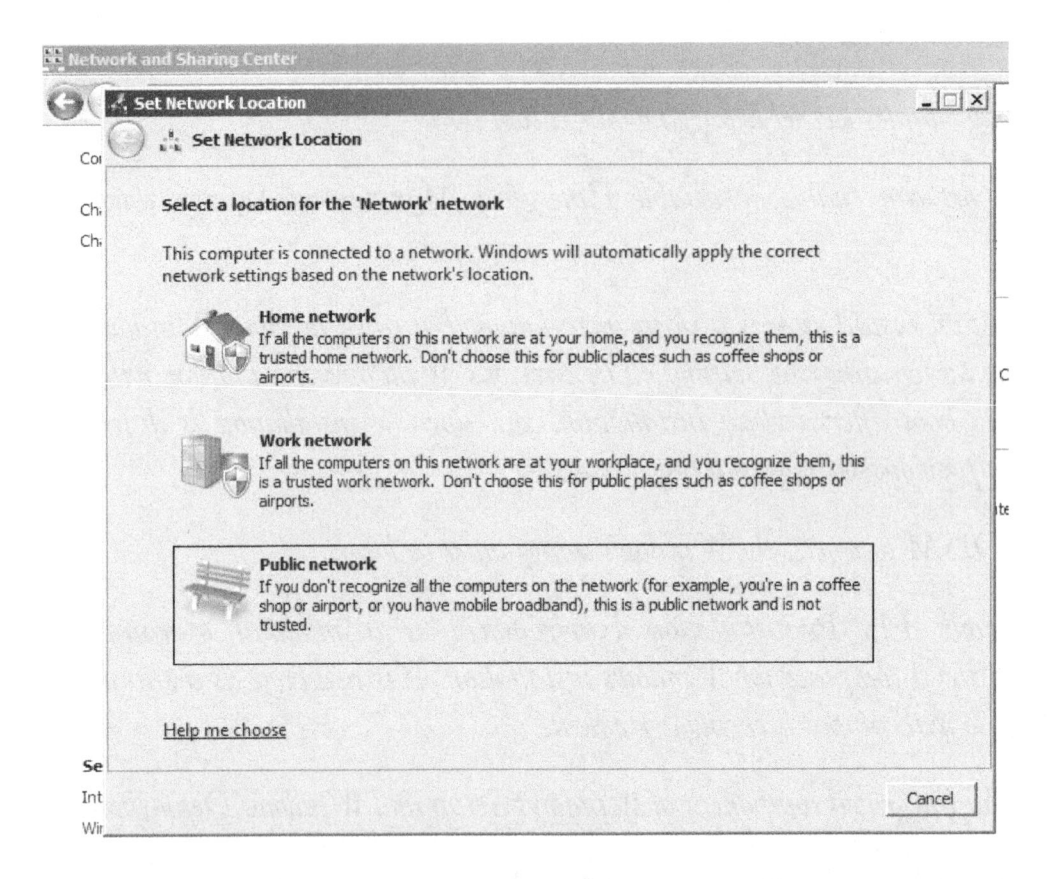

**Network location is a profile containing a collection of network and sharing settings which can be applied to the network you are connected to.** Windows Server has 3 different types of network categories, which are Public, Private and Domain-authenticated. The Set Network Location dialog provides 3 network locations, which are Public, Work and Home. Domain networks by default are automatically set to the Domain Authenticated category. In fact, connecting a computer to a domain network will automatically set the network category to domain authenticated.

Private category, on the other hand, is divided into Work and Home locations, which are primarily for internal Windows configuration. Note that on a domain-joined computer changing the network location will not require administrative privileges. However, on a non-domain-joined computer changing the network location will require administrative privileges.

Network Location and Windows Firewall are in theory mutually independent. In practice, however, the configuration of Windows Firewall would largely be based on the current network category or categories. When connected to a Public network, only Core Networking rules will be enabled. However, when connected to a Private network, rules of Core Networking, Network Discovery, and Remote Assistance are all enabled.

## IP v4 and v6

Windows Server 2008 R2 supports both IPv4 and IPv6. Both of them are installed and enabled by default. It is possible to tunnel IPv6 traffic through an IPv4 network. It is also possible to tunnel IPv4 traffic across an IPv6 network.

There are transition technologies you may consider if you are not ready for IPv6 entirely. ISATAP allows unicast communication between IPv6/IPv4 hosts across your IPv4 intranet. 6to4 allows unicast communication to take place between IPv6/IPv4 hosts and IPv6-capable sites through the Internet. Teredo is similar to 6to4 and can work even when there are private IPv4 addresses and NAT devices involved. IP-HTTPS permits IPv6 to be tunneled using HTTP with SSL as a transport.

# Network Sharing and Discovery

The Network and Sharing Center is an interface for basic networking setup. Network discovery, connection status and file sharing are all available here.

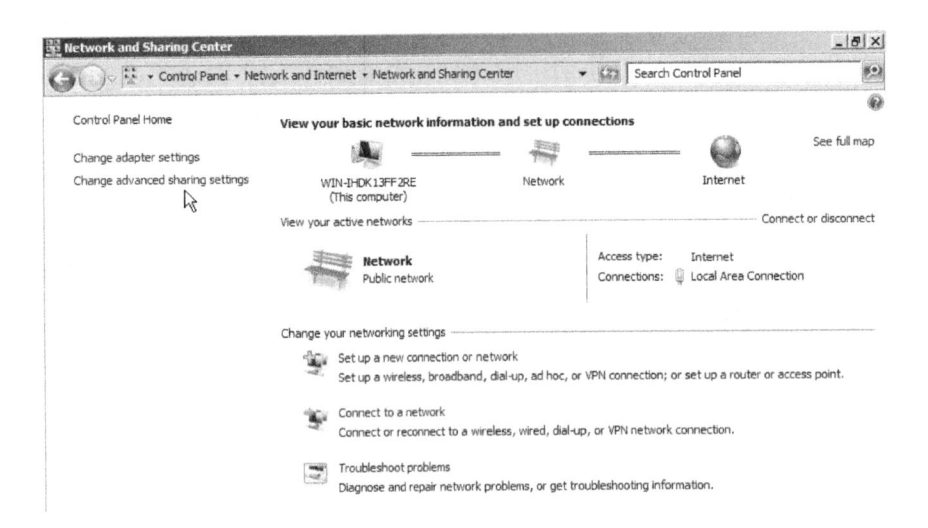

Status of the network adaptors can be viewed by right clicking on the desired adaptor and choose status. Initial troubleshooting can be performed via the Diagnose option.

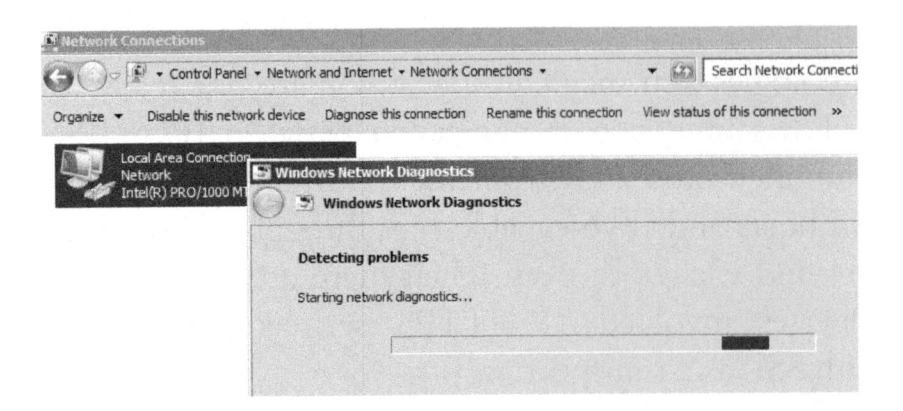

Before you may share files and folders, first you must log in as an Administrator and must make sure that all the relevant systems are connected on the same workgroup. To view the workgroup of the client computer, open the Computer Properties dialog from its Control Panel.

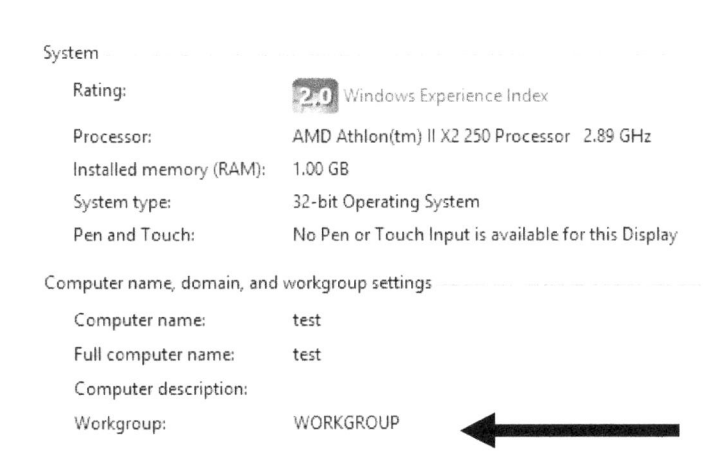

In fact you can always change the computer name and the workgroup name from there:

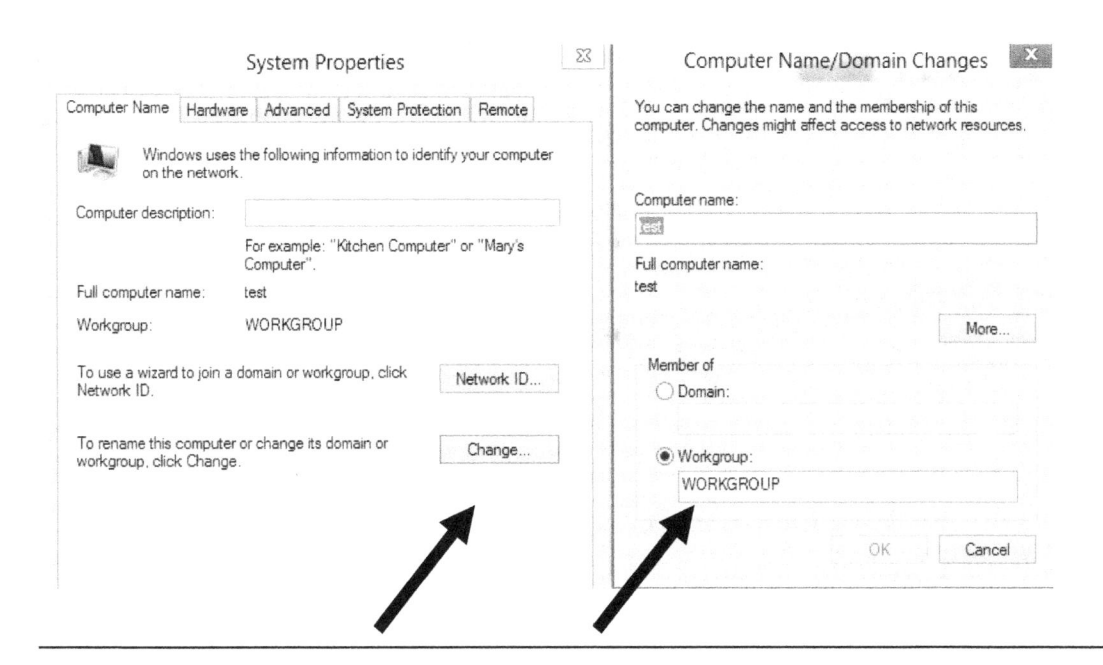

Network Discovery allows the computer to automatically search for other devices on the network. It also works the other around - other computers on the same network can find your computer. An On state allows your computer to see other network computers and devices and also allows people on other network computers to see you. An Off state prevents your computer from seeing others and also prevents people on other network computers from seeing you. A custom state is a mixed state. When you have Network Discovery enabled, the Windows OS becomes immediately discoverable on the network although it would not allow other computers to communicate or access information stored in it. To make the computer accessible from the network, you need to manually enable File and Printer Sharing.

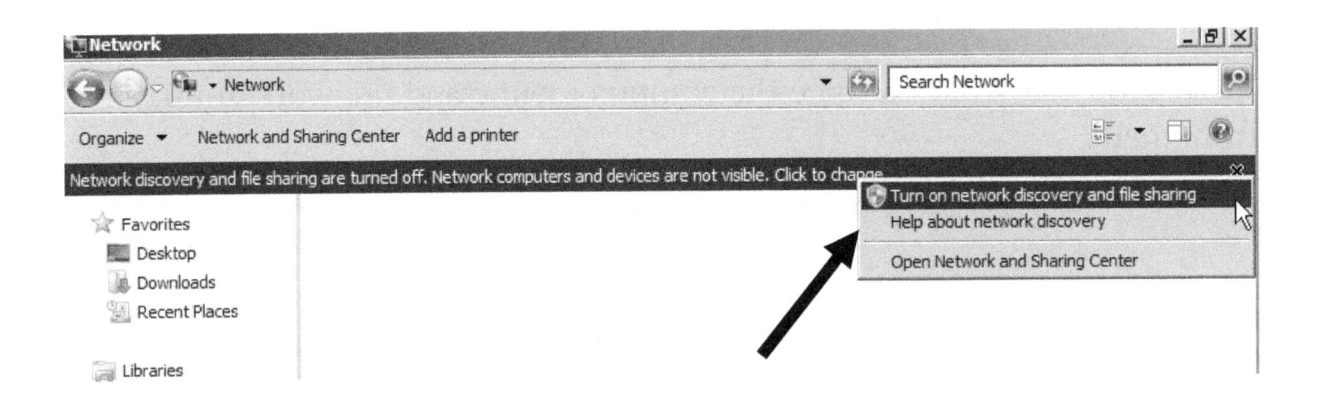

**File and Print Services**

The File Server Resource Manager MMC snap-in can be used to manage storage resources on local or remote servers. You may set soft or hard space limits on a volume or folder tree. OR you may create and apply quota templates with standard quota properties. You may create filter rules to block attempts by users to save certain file types on a volume or folder tree. You may even create and apply screening templates as needed. There are also built-in reports for tracking quota usage, file screening activity, and patterns of storage use.

The File Services role also comes with the Storage Manager for SANs, which can be used to create and manage logical unit numbers on Fibre Channel and Internet SCSI disk drive subsystems that support Virtual Disk Service V1.1 or later. Support for Distributed File System DFS is also available. DFS Namespaces allows you to group shared folders that are located on different servers into one or more logically structured namespaces, while DFS Replication allows you to keep folders synchronized between servers across very sow and weak network connections.

With the Print Services role in place, it is possible to use Print Management with Group Policy to automatically deploy printer connections. Per-user printer connections during background Group Policy refresh operations is fully supported assuming you have Vista or later as the client side OS. You may use the Printer Migration Wizard or the Printbrm.exe utility to export print queues, printer settings, printer ports, and language monitors, and later import them onto another older print server for backward compatibility support.

You can use the Share and Storage Management console to manage shared sessions and files in real time – you can see who is using your share/file in real time and terminate any session as needed.

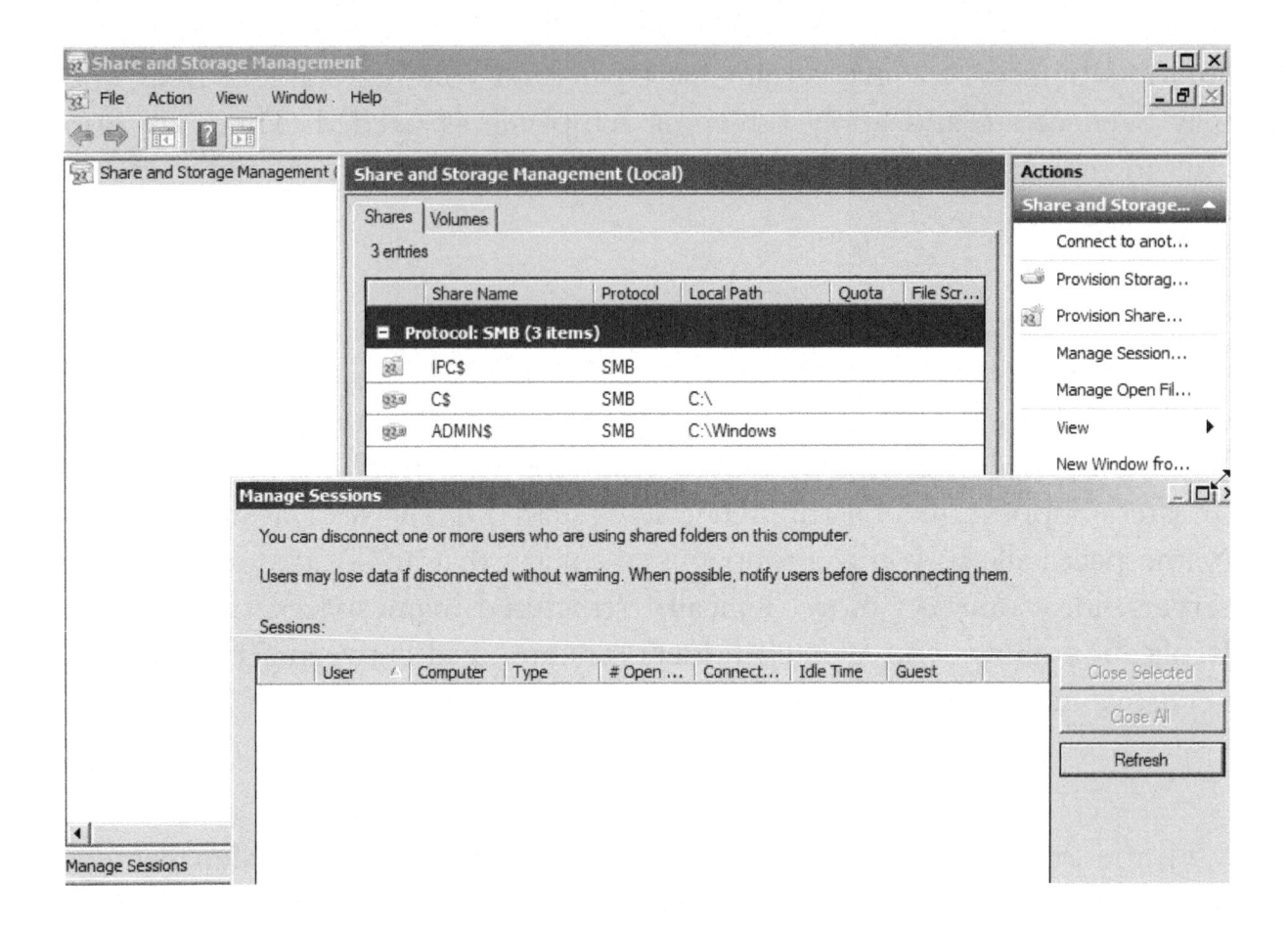

## Name Resolution

Windows Server name resolution can take place via these methods:

- local hosts file located in C:\Windows\System32\drivers\etc\
- DNS lookup
- Link-Local Multicast Name Resolution LLMNR
- NetBIOS name query request within a small network

The hosts file holds a list of ip addresses and the corresponding host name. The file needs to be updated by hand on a per machine basis, which is not preferable. LLMNR is a Microsoft protocol for those private networks that have no DNS server. It can allow private networks to operate as IP networks without requiring the various hosts within it to be configured with addresses. It works by sending multicasts UDP messages via port 5355. Since it requires hosts to transmit multicast LLMNR packets which identify the hosts, security may be at risk. You may use Group policy to disable LLMNR. You may also edit the registry to achieve the same. NetBIOS should only be treated as a measure for very small network or for backward compatibility.

## Command line networking tools

Command line tools such as ipconfig, ping, tracert …etc remain the same across Windows versions. When used with the /all option the ipconfig tool can show a detailed configuration report for all interfaces, wired and wireless. /flushdns is an option that can delete the DNS name cache. /registerdns is an option that can refresh all DHCP leases and even re-register the DNS names. /displaydns is an option that can show the contents of the DNS resolver cache. /release and /renew are options that you can use to release and renew the DHCP-allocated IP address. /renew6 is for renewing IPv6 DHCP lease. You do need to specify the adaptor you are referring to when renewing address leases. Nslookup is for troubleshooting DNS problems, particularly host name resolution. You may in fact set the local computer into the debug mode by using set debug or set d2. The latter gives even more details. Tracert is a route tracing tool capable of showing a list of near-side only router interfaces along the path between a source and a destination. It uses the IP TTL field in the ICMP Echo Requests and ICMP Time Exceeded messages to determine the correct path. For it to work as expected you may need to turn off ICMP filtering. The ping command can send an ICMP Echo Request to a destination IP address. It is the most basic tool for determining connectivity.

```
C:\Users\mike>ping 127.0.0.1
Pinging 127.0.0.1 with 32 bytes of data:
Reply from 127.0.0.1: bytes=32 time<1ms TTL=128
Reply from 127.0.0.1: bytes=32 time<1ms TTL=128
Reply from 127.0.0.1: bytes=32 time<1ms TTL=128
Reply from 127.0.0.1: bytes=32 time<1ms TTL=128

Ping statistics for 127.0.0.1:
    Packets: Sent = 4, Received = 4, Lost = 0 (0% loss),
Approximate round trip times in milli-seconds:
    Minimum = 0ms, Maximum = 0ms, Average = 0ms

C:\Users\mike>
```

The PathPing tool is a route tracing tool with features from both Ping and Tracert. It has a default number of hops set to 30 plus a default wait time before a time-out set to 3000 milliseconds. Netdiag is an advanced tool you can use to isolate networking and connectivity problems. It offers MANY tests to determine the state of a network client, including:

| | | |
|---|---|---|
| Network Adapter Status | NetWare test | Kerberos Test |
| IP Configuration | IPX test | LDAP Test |
| Domain Membership | IPSec test | Route test |
| Transports Test | WINS Service Test | NetStat test |
| APIPA Address | Winsock Test | Bindings test |
| IP Loopback Ping | DNS Test | WAN test |
| Default Gateway | Redirector and Browser Test | Modem test |

| NetBT Name Test | DC Discovery Test | NetWare test |
| | DC List Test | IPX test |
| | Trust Relationship Test | IPSec test |

## Windows Firewall and IP Security Policy

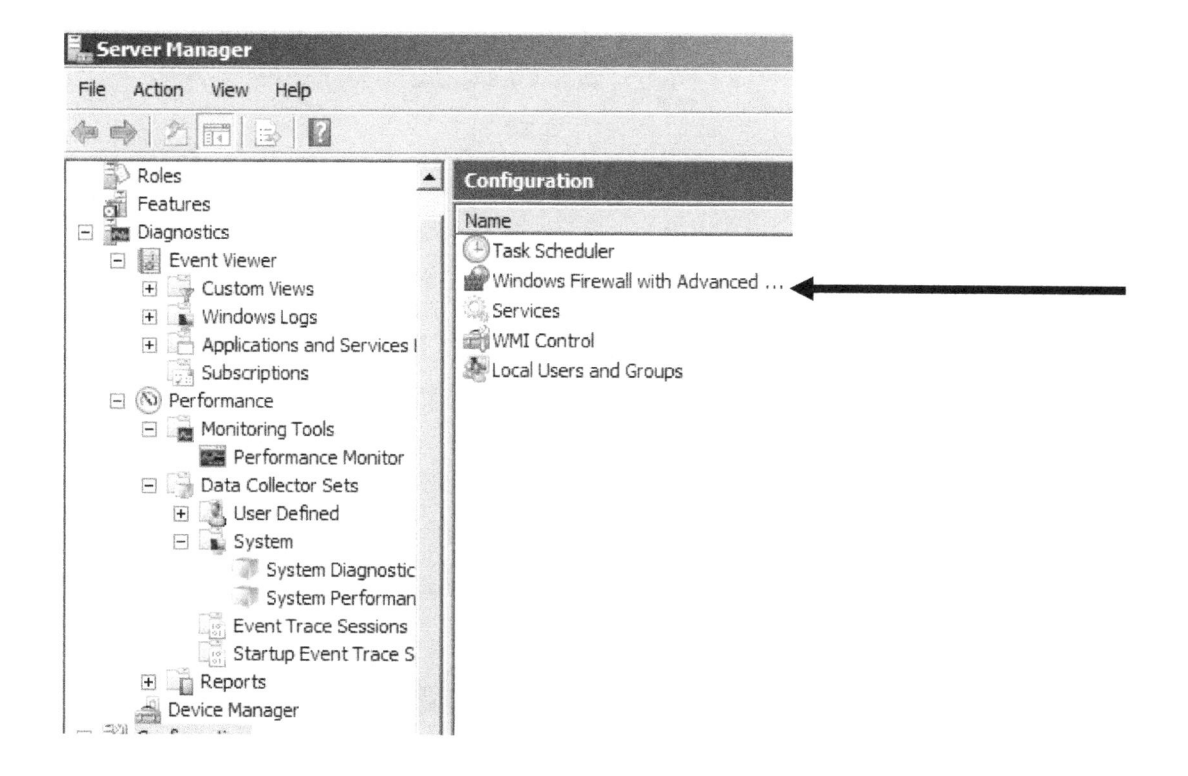

As a stateful host-based firewall, Windows Firewall can be configured via the Windows Firewall with Advanced Security MMC snap-in or the Netsh advfirewall command. You may also access it via the Control Panel. However, configuration via the Control Panel is mostly for typical end user tasks. Advanced tasks should be performed via the MMC snap-in.

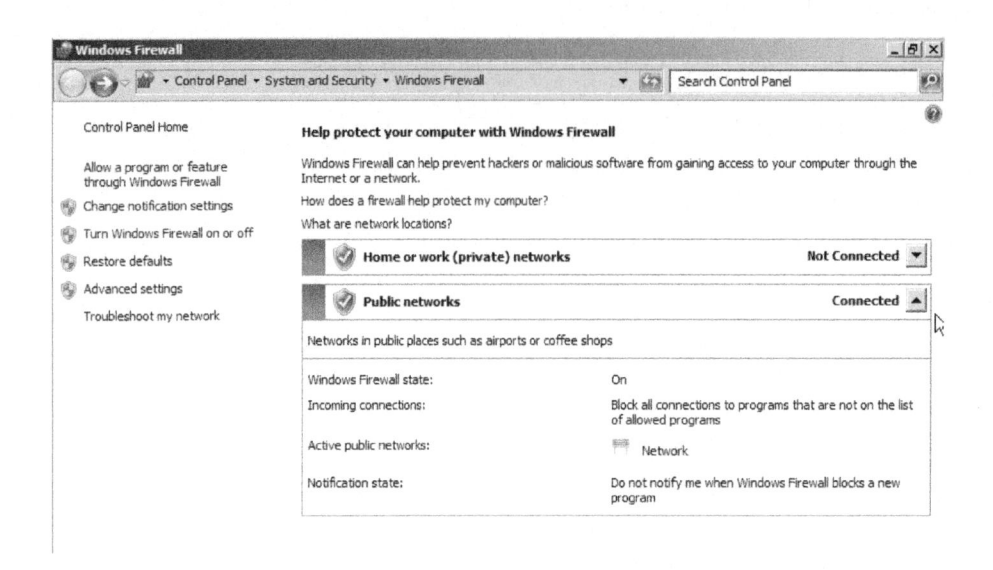

You should determine what windows services and third party programs should be allowed to communicate between different network locations.

At the netsh advfirewall context, the firewall sub command allows you to change to the Netsh AdvFirewall Firewall context so you can view, create, and modify firewall rules. The possible commands are add, delete, set and show. Direction of traffic is either in or out, while action can be allow, block or bypass. On the other hand, if you invoke the command mainmode at the netsh advfirewall context, you can change to the netsh advfirewall mainmode context for viewing, creating, and modifying main mode rules that deal with how IPsec negotiates security associations between computers.

You use firewall rules to allow the server computer to send traffic to, or receive traffic from, programs, system services, computers, or users. Firewall rules can be created to allow the connection, allow a connection only if it is secured through IPsec, or block the connection entirely.

Rules may be for either inbound traffic or outbound traffic and may specify the computers or users, program, service, port, protocol and the type of network adapter involved. In fact it is possible for you to configure a firewall rule to be applied only if the IPv4/IPv6 addresses involved match certain specified local and remote addresses.

The default rule processing behavior is to block all unsolicited inbound network traffic and at the same time allowing all outbound network traffic. You may change the default behavior for the Domain Profile, Private Profile, and Public Profile. Do note that you may use program rules to allow unsolicited incoming traffic through the Windows Firewall only if the program uses Winsock for making port assignments.

There are three profiles for Windows Firewall with Advanced Security, which are Domain (to be applied to a network adapter when it is connected to a network on which it can find a domain controller), Private (to be applied to a network adapter when it is connected to a network identified as a private network behind a security device), and Public. When the profile is not Domain or Private, the default would be Public. With Windows Server 2008 R2, multiple active per-network adapter profiles can be supported.

Firewall rules are either locally stored or save in GPOs. The Windows Service Hardening rule can restrict services from establishing connections in ways not intended out of the box. Connection security rules define authentication using IPsec and enforce Network Access Protection NAP policy.

Authenticated bypass rules allow connections and bypass other inbound rules when the traffic is protected with IPsec. Block rules aim to explicitly blocks a particular type of traffic, and can be used to override a matching allow rule. Allow rules can explicitly allow a particular type of traffic. Default rules define the kind of action to take when a connection does not meet any of the higher order rules. Within each rule category, rules are matched by the specificity - the more specific rules get applied.

IP Security Policies can be created via the Local Policy Editor. There is an IP Security Policy snap-in for backward compatibility. You may use it to create IPsec policies that can be applied to computers running Vista, Windows Server 2008, Windows 7, and Windows Server 2008 R2, although the newest security algorithms and features are not supported.

107

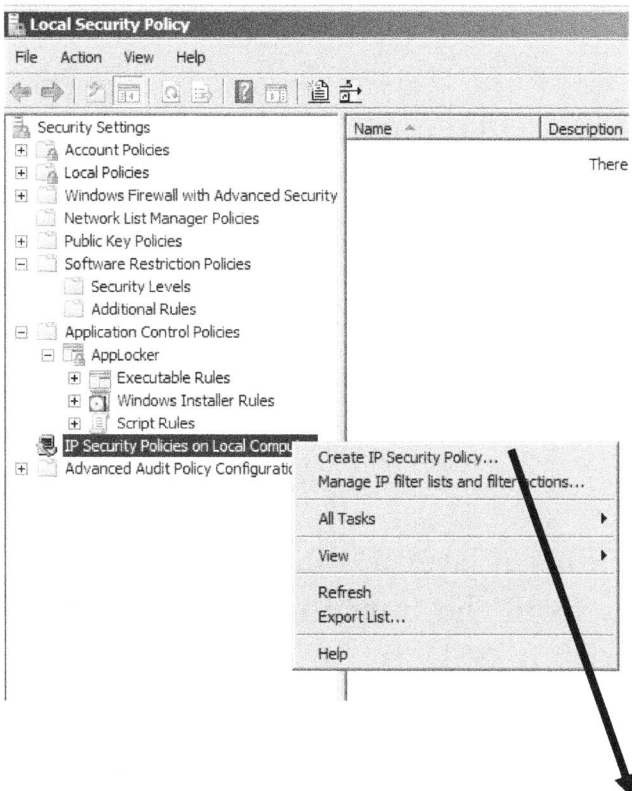

## IPSec and SSL

To prevent messages from being intercepted during transmission over the network, technologies like IPSec and SSL should be considered. They make it very time consuming to hack. Frankly, attackers love to attack a weak spot in a system than to touch a heavily fortified component. They are not likely to attack encrypted information communicated in a network because it would be VERY time consuming. Instead, the endpoints (e.g. the servers and the clients) are often the much easier targets.

IPsec is different from SSL in that it runs at layer 3, so it can protect both TCP and UDP traffic. SSL operates from the transport layer up so less flexibility can be offered. The goal of SSL is to provide endpoint authentication as well as communications privacy via cryptography.

## Disk based encryption

Whole Disk Encryption protects all data on an entire computer disk drive. The engine behinds it operates at the system level that is between the operating system and the disk drive, thus providing totally transparent sector-by-sector disk encryption in background. There are commercial software for this purpose. Windows also offer the EFS Encryption File System for similar use. EFS does support encryption on a per folder basis.

When you choose to encrypt the parent folder, all files and subfolders that are to be added in the future will be encrypted. When you choose to encrypt all files and subfolders when you encrypt a folder, all files and subfolders currently in the folder as well as any files and subfolders that are to be added in the future will be encrypted. When you choose to encrypt the folder only, files and subfolders currently in the folder will not be encrypted.

Encrypting File System certificates allow the certificate holder to use EFS to encrypt and decrypt data. Ordinary EFS users should be granted this type of certificate. File Recovery certificates are for recovering encrypted files and folders. Domain admins and/or designated data recovery agents should be granted this type of certificate. You should use the Certificates MMC snap-in to back up the default recovery keys. Do so before you make any changes to the default recovery policy!

**Firewall security**

Firewall configuration, administration and operational procedures should always be well documented. Configuration of multiple firewalls used in parallel (if any) must be identical. Integrity checking of the configuration files of the firewall using checksums should be performed whenever applicable. Log recording and review for the firewall should be done regularly. Backups of the system and configuration files for firewall must be regularly taken. And keep in mind, proper maintenance of user accounts is highly important.

You must be aware that firewall is never the totality of a security solution. There are a number of threats that a firewall cannot protect against, including:

- Denial of service attacks and assure data integrity
- Attacks from unwitting users
- Attacks from computer virus or malicious code

On the other hand you want to know that the boundary between firewall and other security measures is becoming increasingly blurred as firewall manufacturers continuously incorporate additional features. A lot of the modern routers, for example, are having basic firewall functions and features. Always remember, routers should be properly configured to deny all traffic by default, and to allow only permitted traffic to go through. Source routing should be disabled. Logging, backup and other administrative tasks should be properly performed similar to those for the firewall.

**Virus security**

Virus always poses a problem, and you may need a separate host machine to be set up to connect with the firewall to check for computer viruses and malicious codes in all incoming traffic when going through the firewall. This can centralize the control in updating individual computer virus and/or malicious code patterns, and prevent the computer virus or malicious codes from entering into the web or mail servers. Anti-virus software and malicious code detection and repair software may as well be incorporated with the mail server or the web server to specifically protect individual servers.

**Windows Firewall does not stop viruses!**

**Web server security**

If you are running Web Servers, separate web servers should be used to restrict access when providing different information to internal and external users. Web servers may be placed inside or outside the internal network. Web servers, which are placed inside the internal network, are normally used for providing information to internal users, while outside servers are used for disseminating information to the public or external users. All outside web servers need to be connected to the firewall in the DMZ with a separate network interface. Ideally a dedicated host should be assigned for running a web server, a mail server or any critical service. The reason is simple - in case of being compromised, this can reduce the impact to other services.

**IIS is always vulnerable to attacks!**

### Name resolution security

All host names and addresses stored in an external DNS are supposed to be exposed to public. Hence, the external DNS should not hold information about the internal network. The external DNS may also be hosted at the ISP. A separate internal DNS server should be set up and placed in the internal network if internal domain information need not be disclosed to the Internet.

### Remote Management

Remote Desktop RDP is a feature that allows one to connect to the work computer from a remote location, exactly like using VNC. On the client side, to enable the remote desktop connection feature on a typical client such as Windows 7 so the computer can accept incoming request, click Start -> right click the Computer option -> Properties -> Remote settings -> System

Properties -> Allow connections from computers running any version of Remote Desktop. To initiate a connection, choose Start -> All Programs -> Accessories -> Remote Desktop Connection. You need to provide the destination IP address, user name and password.

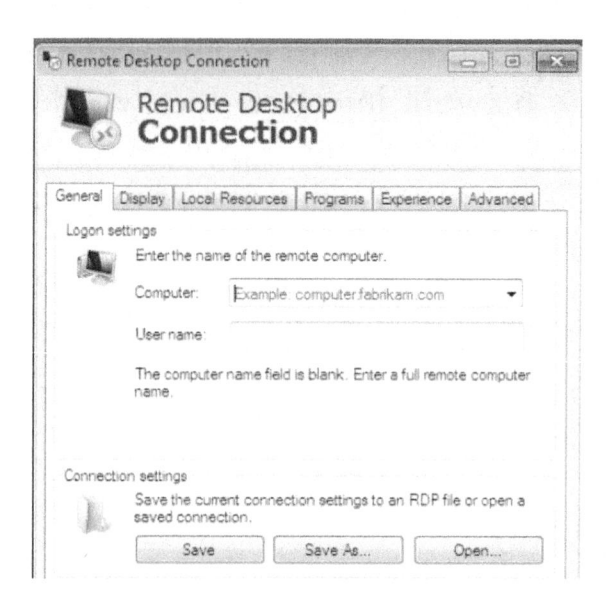

Do note that Remote Desktop is usually not enabled by default on the client. Also, if your remote connection is behind a router or a firewall, make sure connections on port 3389 are allowed. If you want to perform remote server management from Windows 7, you should consider to use the Remote Server Administration Tools RSAT. Through the RSAT tools you can manage computers running Server 2008 R2, Server 2008, or Server 2003. By default the tools would only open those ports and enables only those services that are required for remote management to function.

SERVER SIDE - To install and configure a Remote Desktop Session Host RD Session Host server, you need to add the RD Session Host role service to your Windows Server 2008 R2 computer. You can use Server Manager to achieve this. For your users to connect to this server, don't forget to add the user accounts to the local Remote Desktop Users group. In fact, you can configure a remote desktop services profile for each individual user account:

The Remote Desktop Gateway RD Gateway role service can allow authorized remote users to connect to those RDP accessible resources hosted on the internal corporate networks from Remote Desktop Connection RDC client. When planning to use this role keep in mind that response time would be the key metric for performance measurement. It tells the time taken for a data packet to travel from the RDC through the

Gateway server to the RD Session Host server and then return back to the RDC.

**Folder Redirection and Offline Access**

Folder redirection allows users and administrators to redirect the path of a folder to a new location. Redirection can be done either manually or through using Group Policy. The new location can be a local folder or a directory somewhere on the network.

On the CLIENT SIDE - In Windows 7, synchronization of offline files take place automatically in the background so there is no need to manually choose between online and offline modes. Windows 7 is capable of redirecting user folders to the proper network location and automatically synchronizes the files. When the user logs off the network, Windows 7 will open the local copies instead. You need to share the folder on the server before you can enable caching for offline file operation. You also need to enable caching on the client computer by mapping a network drive or browsing the network for locating the shared folder. You can right click on the folder and choose "Always Available Offline."

On the SERVER SIDE - You can configure Offline Files through the Offline Files policies GPO. Four of the policies are particularly useful (based on their names you should know their meanings):

- Subfolders always available offline

- Limit disk space used by offline files
- Allow or Disallow use of the Offline Files feature
- Encrypt the Offline Files cache

If sync conflicts occur due to the fact that changes are made to files available offline both on the file server and on the local cache, you will need to use the Sync Center to get them resolved. You can choose to keep the local version, keep the server version or keep both versions, with the local copy being renamed.

Offline Files can make network files available even when a network connection to the server is either unavailable or is very slow. In any case, based on MS' recommendation, you should create a root share on the server and then let the system create the users' folders, then synchronize files at logoff when using Folder Redirection with Offline Files. Since the redirected folders may contain personal information, you want to create a security group for those users who have redirected folders on a particular share and accordingly limit access only to those users. You want to create a hidden share by using a dollar sign ($) after the share name. And you should only grant users the minimum permissions necessary for accessing the data. Do not rely only on EFS. EFS can encrypt files on a remote server only while it is stored on the disk, but not when it is transmitted across the network. You do want to encrypt the offline file cache. You can do so via Group Policy - check out the Computer Configuration\Administrative Templates\Network\Offline Files node in the Group Policy Object Editor snap-in. OR, click Folder Options on the Tools menu from within Windows Explorer. Click on Offline Files, and then check the Encrypt offline files to secure data check box.

## DirectAccess, Remote Access and Routing

DirectAccess aims to allow connectivity to the corporate network without the need for using traditional VPN connections. It supports domain-joined Windows 7 Enterprise and Ultimate edition clients as well as Windows 8 clients. Earlier clients are not supported.

A complete DirectAccess solution for mobile access requires a DirectAccess server running Windows Server 2008 R2 with dual network adapters - one facing the internet another facing the intranet. The former needs to have two consecutive public IPv4 addresses assigned. There must also be a domain controller and DNS server running Windows Server 2008 SP2 or Windows Server 2008 R2, plus a public key infrastructure issuing computer certificates. The client computers must be running Windows 7 Enterprise or Windows 7 Ultimate and must be members of the AD DS domain. Think of it as a better and user friendlier way of using VPN for remote connections.

DirectAccess makes use of IPsec for authentication (in fact, authentication takes place before the user logs on) and encryption of communications across the Internet. A major requirement for DirectAccess to work is that IPv6 must be implemented. If IPv6 is not yet deployed, you will need to use transition technologies. You may also use a NAT64 device to translate IPv6 and IPv4 traffics. When there is a firewall or proxy server that prevents the client from using 6to4 or Teredo to reach the DirectAccess server, the client will automatically connect via IP-HTTPS. You may use Nltest.exe at the command line with the options /dsgetdc: /force for DirectAccess troubleshooting. You may determine whether DirectAccess clients,

DirectAccess servers, and other intranet resources can actually contact your domain controllers for IPsec authentication. Do note that the DirectAccess Management Console is a feature that has to be manually installed. It is not installed by default.

Select one or more features to install on this server.
Features:
- [ ] .NET Framework 3.5.1 Features
- [ ] Background Intelligent Transfer Service (BITS)
- [ ] BitLocker Drive Encryption
- [ ] BranchCache
- [ ] Connection Manager Administration Kit
- [ ] Desktop Experience
- [ ] DirectAccess Management Console ←

The Microsoft DirectAccess Connectivity Assistant DCA as part of the Windows Optimized Desktop Toolkit 2010 is a tool that can inform mobile users of their connectivity status and provide tools to help them reconnect if necessary. It can also create diagnostics to ease the troubleshooting problem.

The Routing and Remote Access service RRAS has two major functions. It allows you to deploy VPN connections to provide end users with remote access to the corporate network. It also allows you to create a site-to-site VPN connection between two servers. On the other hand, it allows your server to act as a software router and/or a network address translator.

In Windows Server 2008 R2, a server computer may be configured to run with the RRAS server role. Packet filtering on a given interface is possible, and can be enabled via Windows firewall or inbound/outbound filters of

RRAS. Don't use both together. The RRAS Packet Filter is a stateless mechanism. It is configurable through the RRAS MMC snap-in, the netsh based scripting mechanism or the remote access policies.

To install RRAS, through Server Manager you go to Roles Summary and click Add roles. When selecting Server Roles, choose Network Policy and Access Services. Then pick Routing and Remote Access Services. After installing the RRAS server role, it is initially in a disabled state so you must enable it manually.

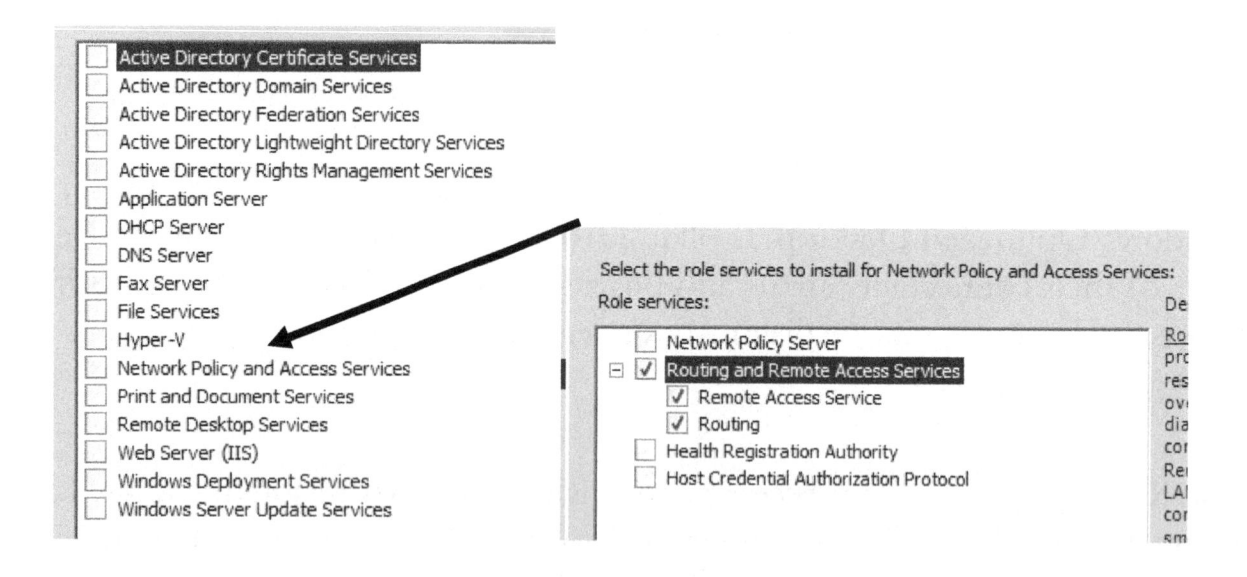

From within the RRAS MMC Snap-in you should right click on the server name and click Configure and Enable Routing and Remote Access. This will call up the configuration wizard for it.

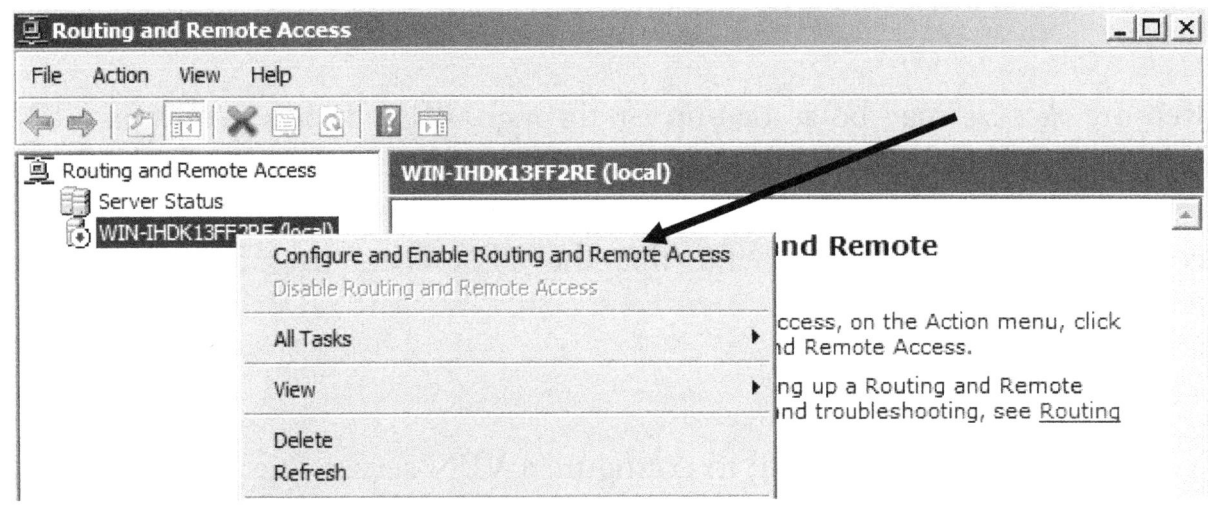

**Routing and Remote Access**

File   Action   View   Help

| Routing and Remote Access | WIN-IHDK13FF2RE (local) |

Server Status
WIN-IHDK13FF2RE (local)

Configure and Enable Routing and Remote Access
Disable Routing and Remote Access
All Tasks
View
Delete
Refresh

nd Remote

ccess, on the Action menu, click
nd Remote Access.

ng up a Routing and Remote
nd troubleshooting, see Routing

---

**Routing and Remote Access Server Setup Wizard**

**Welcome to the Routing and Remote Access Server Setup Wizard**

This wizard helps you set up your server so that you can connect to other networks and allow connections from remote clients.

To continue, click Next.

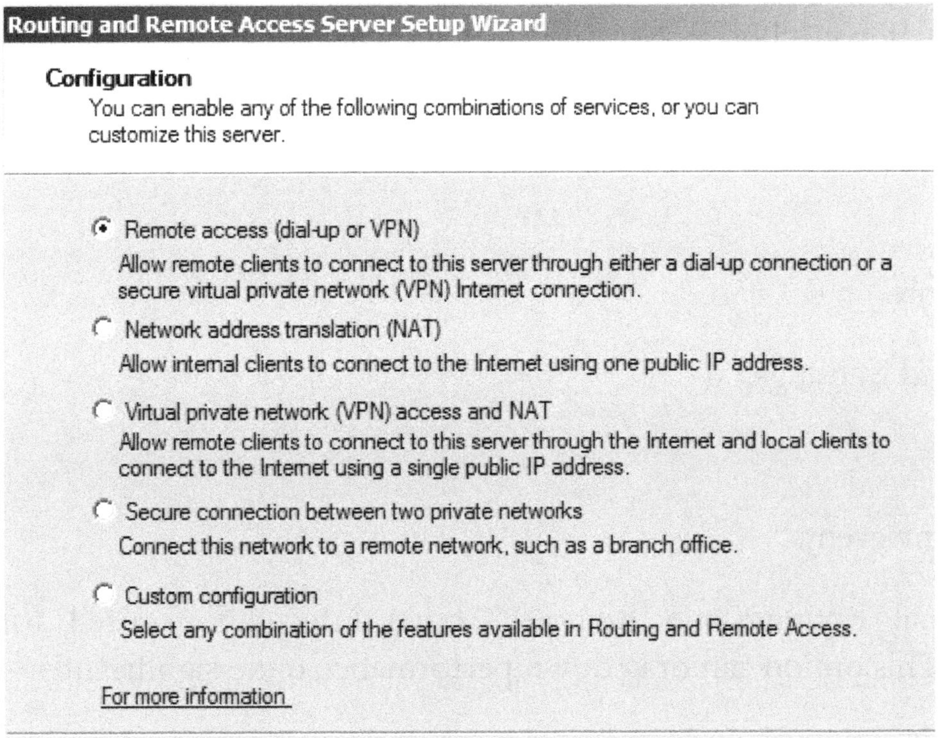

---

**Routing and Remote Access Server Setup Wizard**

**Configuration**
You can enable any of the following combinations of services, or you can customize this server.

(•) Remote access (dial-up or VPN)
Allow remote clients to connect to this server through either a dial-up connection or a secure virtual private network (VPN) Internet connection.

( ) Network address translation (NAT)
Allow internal clients to connect to the Internet using one public IP address.

( ) Virtual private network (VPN) access and NAT
Allow remote clients to connect to this server through the Internet and local clients to connect to the Internet using a single public IP address.

( ) Secure connection between two private networks
Connect this network to a remote network, such as a branch office.

( ) Custom configuration
Select any combination of the features available in Routing and Remote Access.

For more information

Remote Access may be as dial-up or through VPN. If it serves as a VPN server, remember that it needs a machine certificate to create SSL VPN connection with the SSL VPN client, and that the common name on the certificate must match the name that the VPN client uses for making the connection.

You should NOT use DHCP to configure a VPN server. It is recommended that you manually configure TCP/IP or use DHCP with MAC address reservations so that the TCP/IP configuration of the VPN server can be kept stable.

In terms of user authentication, through the Managing Multiple Remote Access Servers page you may select whether you want to use a centralized RADIUS server. If you choose No, then RRAS will use its local account database or the domain account database if it is a member of AD. In terms of logging, these are the available options:

- Log errors only.
- Log errors and warnings.
- Log all events.
- Do not log any events.
- Log additional Routing and Remote Access information (used for debugging). This option can drag down performance quite significantly.

To allow RRAS to function as a router, you should enable and configure RIP via the RRAS MMC snap-in. For IPv4, RIP Version 2 for Internet Protocol is the choice. You should add it, then right-click RIP and choose New Interface. You should select the interface that is connected to a subnet on which the remote router is connected so your interface can communicate with it through RIP. For security purpose you want to be careful about accpeting routing updates from other routers. Possible options are:

- Accept announcements from all routers - this is the default.
- Accept announcements from listed routers only - recommended.
- Ignore announcements from all listed routers

RRAS supports NAT. HOWEVER, since NAT already includes addressing and name resolution features that provide DHCP and DNS services to clients, you should not run DHCP service or DHCP Relay Agent with NAT addressing enabled. You should also NOT run the DNS service if NAT TCP/IP networking name resolution is currently enabled.

## BranchCache

BranchCache is officially a WAN bandwidth optimization technology. In fact it is nothing other than a smart file caching service. With it, after a client has downloaded a piece of content, other clients that look for the same content can retrieve content information identifiers and accordingly find the content in the local office where the content is cached. Hosted cache mode is for branch office with a cache server while distributed cache mode is for a server-less environment. Types of content server include File server, Web server and Application server.

Do note that BranchCache can be deployed in a domain-based or non-domain based environment, as long as a VPN or DirectAccess connection is available between the content servers and the branch office. Also note that it is NOT a feature installed by default so you must add it yourself.

## Bitlocker

BitLocker is a feature for protecting against unauthorized access to local drive data, including data stored on fixed or removable drives. When a drive is encrypted with BitLocker, the drive can only be unlocked with a password or a smart card credential. In the case where all unlock methods become unsuccessful, you must use a recovery key to regain access to the drive.

BitLocker supports fixed data drive when the drive is formatted with exFAT, FAT16, FAT32, or NTFS and that there is 64 MB of available disk space. To allow the drive to be unlocked automatically by the operating system for normal usage, the operating system drive itself must be protected by BitLocker. Keep in mind, if you want to encrypt the operating system drive, there are special requirements to meet. BitLocker stores its own encryption and decryption key in a hardware device separate from your hard disk so you must have either a computer with a Trusted Platform Module TPM or a removable USB storage device.

Note that for a TPM to be used by BitLocker, it must have a RSA key pair as the endorsement key. Also, the computer must have been configured with a separate active partition to be used as the system partition. To be precise, for BitLocker to operate correctly on operating system drives, you need to have two NTFS partitions, with one for the operating system and another for the system. The system partition needs at least 100 MB for BitLocker. If Windows RE is also there, you need at least 300 MB. This system partition will always remain unencrypted so your computer can start. The partition that holds the operating system can be separately encrypted.

Bitlocker is NOT installed by default so you must add it yourself.

**Questions:**

1. What is network location?

2. Network Location and Windows Firewall are in theory mutually dependent. True?

3. Encryption for File Sharing Connections can be set to ____-bit encryption for the best possible protection.

4. Compare ISATAP with 6to4.

5. IP-HTTPS permits IPv6 to be tunneled using:

6. Which ipconfig option can delete the DNS name cache?

7. Which ipconfig option can refresh all DHCP leases and even re-register the DNS names?

8. Which ipconfig option can show the contents of the DNS resolver cache?

9. Windows Firewall can be configured via what tool or interface?

10. At the netsh advfirewall context, what command allows you to change to the Netsh AdvFirewall Firewall context?

11. The possible commands in the firewall context include:

12. With Windows Firewall, what are the directions of traffic and the possible actions to take?

13. What is the Windows Service Hardening rule?

14. What are connection security rules for?

15. If you want to perform remote server management from Windows 7, what tool should you use?

16. Describe Server Manager.

17. DirectAccess makes use of _____ for authentication.

18. DirectAccess makes use of _____ for encryption of communications across the Internet.

19. A major requirement for DirectAccess to work is that IPv6 must be implemented. True?

20. BitLocker supports fixed data drive when the drive is formatted with:

21. In a Windows domain, which port is required for Remote Assistance to work?

22. Remote Assistance requires a password of what length?

23. BranchCache can be deployed in a domain-based or non-domain based environment as long as what connection is available?

24. You should not run DHCP service or DHCP Relay Agent with NAT addressing enabled due to what reason?

25. You should NOT use DHCP to configure a VPN server. Instead you should:

26. The RRAS Packet Filter is configurable through:


## Answers:

1. *Network location is a profile containing a collection of network and sharing settings which can be applied to the network you are connected to.*

2. *Network Location and Windows Firewall are in theory mutually independent.*

3. Encryption for File Sharing Connections can be set to 128-bit encryption or the weaker 40/56 bit encryption.

4. ISATAP allows unicast communication between IPv6/IPv4 hosts across your IPv4 intranet. 6to4 allows unicast communication to take place between IPv6/IPv4 hosts and IPv6-capable sites through the Internet.

5. IP-HTTPS permits IPv6 to be tunneled using HTTP with SSL as a transport.

6. /flushdns is an option that can delete the DNS name cache.

7. /registerdns is an option that can refresh all DHCP leases and even re-register the DNS names.

8. /displaydns is an option that can show the contents of the DNS resolver cache.

9. Windows Firewall can now be configured via the Windows Firewall with Advanced Security MMC snap-in or the Netsh advfirewall command.

10. At the netsh advfirewall context, the firewall command allows you to change to the Netsh AdvFirewall Firewall context so you can view, create, and modify firewall rules.

11. The possible commands are add, delete, set and show.

12. Direction of traffic is either in or out, while action can be allow, block or bypass.

13. The Windows Service Hardening rule can restrict services from establishing connections in ways not intended out of the box.

14. Connection security rules define authentication using IPsec and enforce Network Access Protection NAP policy.

15. If you want to perform remote server management from Windows 7, you use the Remote Server Administration Tools RSAT.

16. A very useful tool is the Server Manager. When you are a member of the Administrators group, you can manage roles and features on server computer running either the full or Server Core installation options of Server 2008 R2.

17. DirectAccess makes use of IPsec for authentication.

18. DirectAccess makes use of IPsec for encryption of communications across the Internet.

19. A major requirement for DirectAccess to work is that IPv6 must be implemented.

20. BitLocker supports fixed data drive when the drive is formatted with exFAT, FAT16, FAT32, or NTFS and that there is 64 MB of available disk space.

21. In a Windows domain, you can enable the Windows Firewall exception for Remote Assistance so Port 135 TCP can be made open for Remote Assistance to work.

22. The Remote Assistance Wizard can actually create an email or file invitation for remote assistance and also generate a password (an automatically-generated 12-character password) for the necessary session.

23. BranchCache can be deployed in a domain-based or non-domain based environment, as long as a VPN or DirectAccess connection is available between the content servers and the branch office.

24. RRAS supports NAT. HOWEVER, since NAT already includes addressing and name resolution features that provide DHCP and DNS services to clients, you should not run DHCP service or DHCP Relay Agent with NAT addressing enabled.

25. You should NOT use DHCP to configure a VPN server. It is recommended that you manually configure TCP/IP or use DHCP with MAC address reservations so that the TCP/IP configuration of the VPN server can be kept stable.

26. The RRAS Packet Filter is a stateless mechanism. It is configurable through the RRAS MMC snap-in, the netsh based scripting mechanism or the remote access policies.

# System Monitoring, Performance Management and Maintenance

## Event Viewer

Event logging starts automatically when you start Windows Server 2008 R2. You can find Event Viewer via Computer Management or Server Manager:

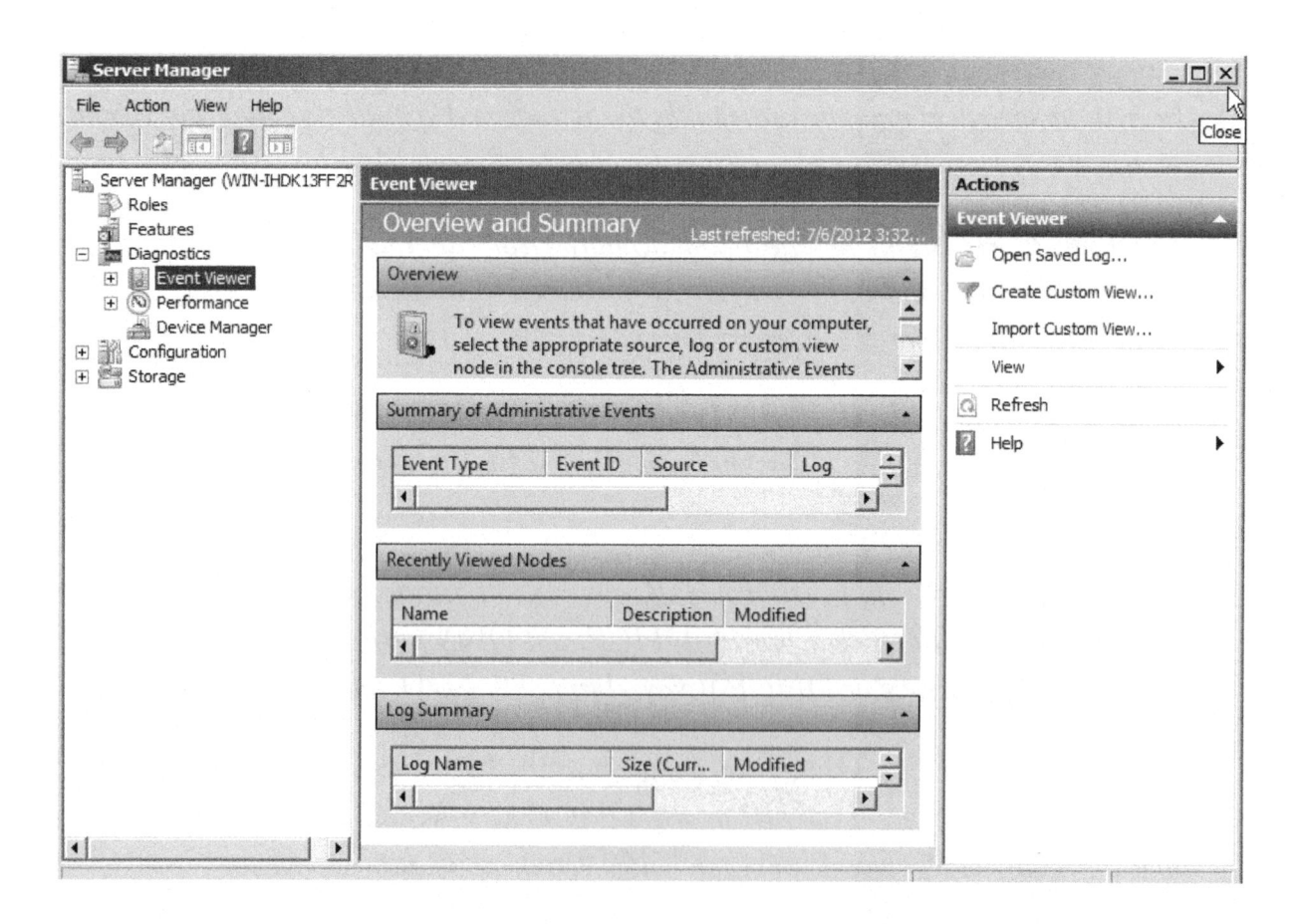

There are different types of application or program events. Hardware events are also under this category. Officially, the types of Applications and Services logs include are Admin, which record problems that directly affect end users; Operational, which may not always indicate problems but simply records of event occurrences; Analytic, which deals with specialized issues with Windows; Debug, which gives records of problems for programmers to solve problems; and Internet Explorer.

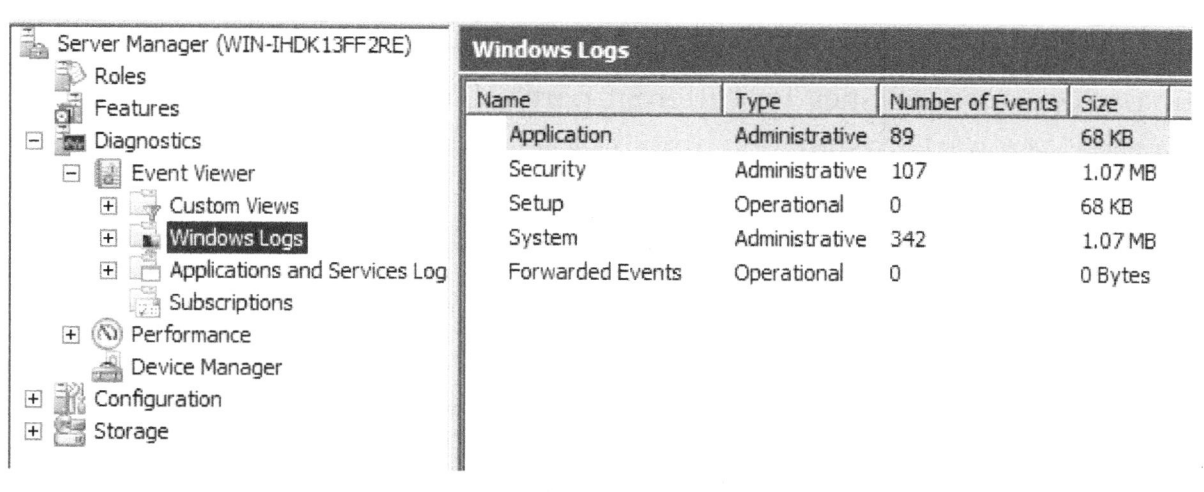

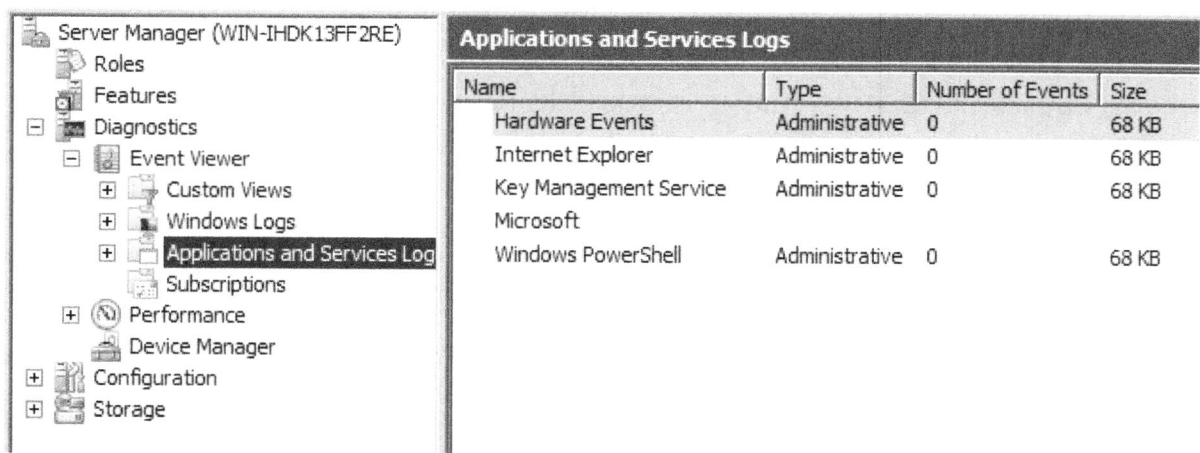

| Windows Logs | | | |
|---|---|---|---|
| Name | Type | Number of Events | Size |
| Application | Administrative | 89 | 68 KB |
| Security | Administrative | 107 | 1.07 MB |
| Setup | Operational | 0 | 68 KB |
| System | Administrative | 342 | 1.07 MB |
| Forwarded Events | Operational | 0 | 0 Bytes |

| Applications and Services Logs | | | |
|---|---|---|---|
| Name | Type | Number of Events | Size |
| Hardware Events | Administrative | 0 | 68 KB |
| Internet Explorer | Administrative | 0 | 68 KB |
| Key Management Service | Administrative | 0 | 68 KB |
| Microsoft | | | |
| Windows PowerShell | Administrative | 0 | 68 KB |

Application or program events are further classified into error, warning, and information depending on their seriousness. An error describes a significant problem. A warning is not yet a significant problem but is likely a problem soon. An information event simply describes successful operation.

Security-related events are audits that describe success or failure of an event. Setup events are for reviewing actions occurred during Windows Setup and the performance statistics for different parts of Windows Setup. The log file is called Setup.etl. System events are logged by Windows and Windows system services. They may be error, warning, or information. Forwarded events are those that have been forwarded to here by other computers on the network. Setup log deals with application setup.

Because events logged are saved in XML format, it is technically possible to construct XML queries to parse the output for display in somewhere else. Do note that it is possible to change the log size and the overwrite behaviors of log entries. Also note that it is possible to collect copies of events from multiple remote computers. To precisely specify the remote to collect, you create an event subscription.

You may use Event Viewer to troubleshoot a problem by locating all events that are related regardless of which event log they appear in. You do this by creating a custom view which can filter for specific events across multiple logs. In Event Viewer, you may choose Action - Create Custom View to achieve this.

It is important for you to control the size of the logs due to the risk of running out of log storage space. You may specify the max log size and what to do if the max size is reached. The possible log retention policies are:

- Overwrite events as needed, meaning new events are continue to be stored when the log file is full, and that each new incoming event will replace the oldest event in the log.

- Archive the log when full without overwriting any events.

- Do not overwrite any events so you must clear the logs manually. You can clear events via the Event Viewer or the wevtutil command line command.

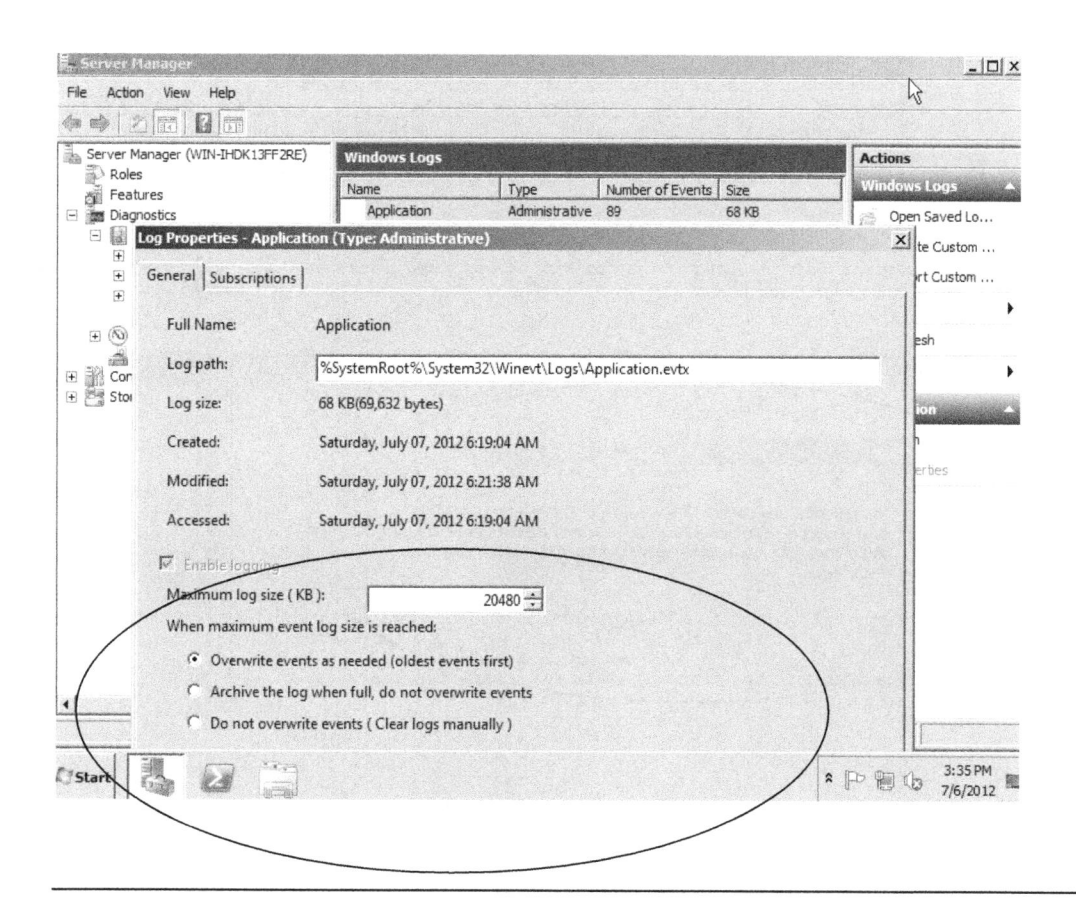

Subscription is all about collecting events from other computers. The Event Collector Service must be made running. Before creating a subscription to collect events on a computer, there is a need to first configure both the collecting computer and the computer from which events will be collected. You need to run the winrm quickconfig command on the source computer. You then need to use the wecutil qc command on the collector computer. Finally you need to add the computer account of the collector computer to the local Administrators group of the source computer.

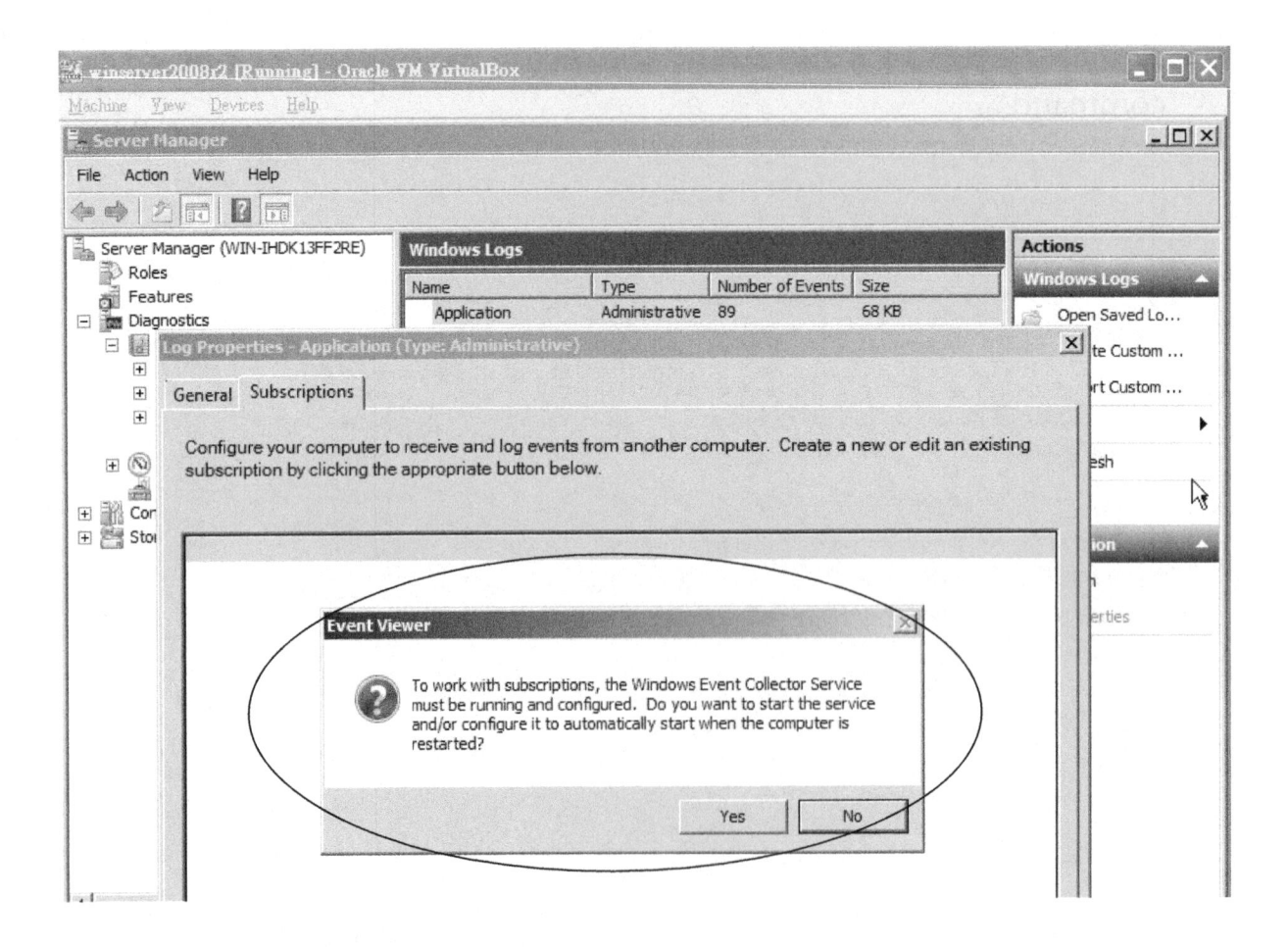

There are different Event Delivery Optimization Options. The Normal option ensures reliable delivery of events without making any attempt to conserve bandwidth. The Minimize Bandwidth option strictly control the use of network bandwidth for event delivery. It makes use of push delivery with a batch timeout of 6 hours. Minimize Latency focuses on event delivery with minimal delay. The batch timeout is set to 30 seconds.

## Perfmon

You can access perfmon via the perfmon.msc (or perfmon.exe through the command line), or through Computer Management / Server Manager. It produces a graphical display of the built-in Windows performance counters in real time using multiple graph views. It also allows you to review historical data. You need to select and add counters for any graph to be produced.

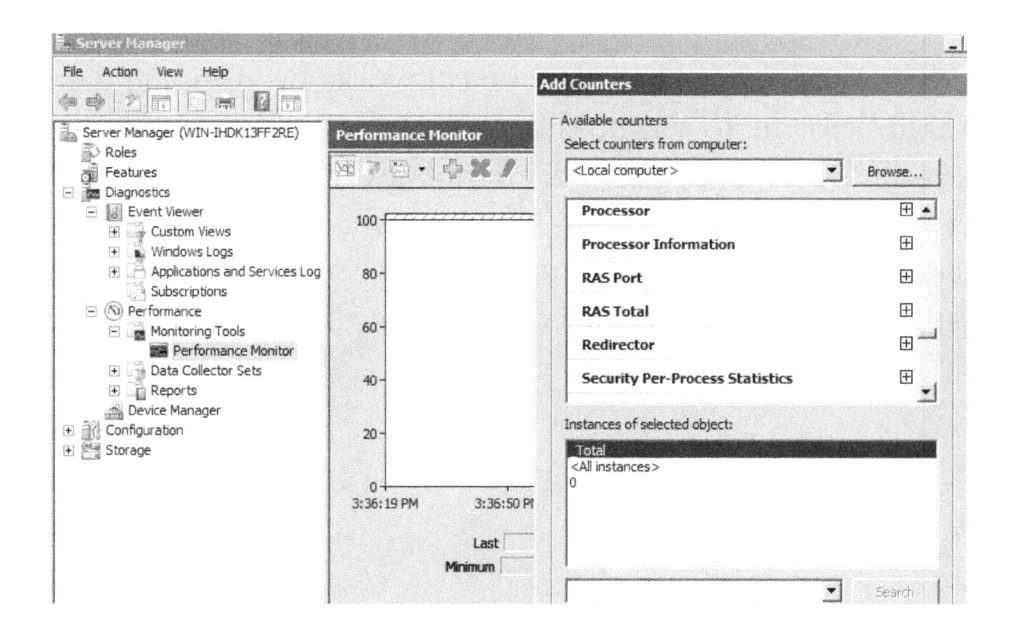

For most performance scenarios, these counters are quite sufficient:

- Memory: % Committed Bytes In Use
- Memory: Page Faults/sec
- PhysicalDisk: Disk Read Bytes/sec
- PhysicalDisk: Disk Reads/sec
- PhysicalDisk: Disk Write Bytes/sec
- PhysicalDisk: Disk Writes/sec
- Processor: % Idle Time
- Processor: Interrupts/sec
- System: Threads

The Data Collector Set is an XML object. The object works by grouping data collectors into reusable elements to fit into different performance monitoring scenarios. The default Data Collector Set templates are for collecting performance data immediately without the need for complicated configuration. If necessary, you may add counters to the various log files and schedule the start, stop, and duration of the collection.

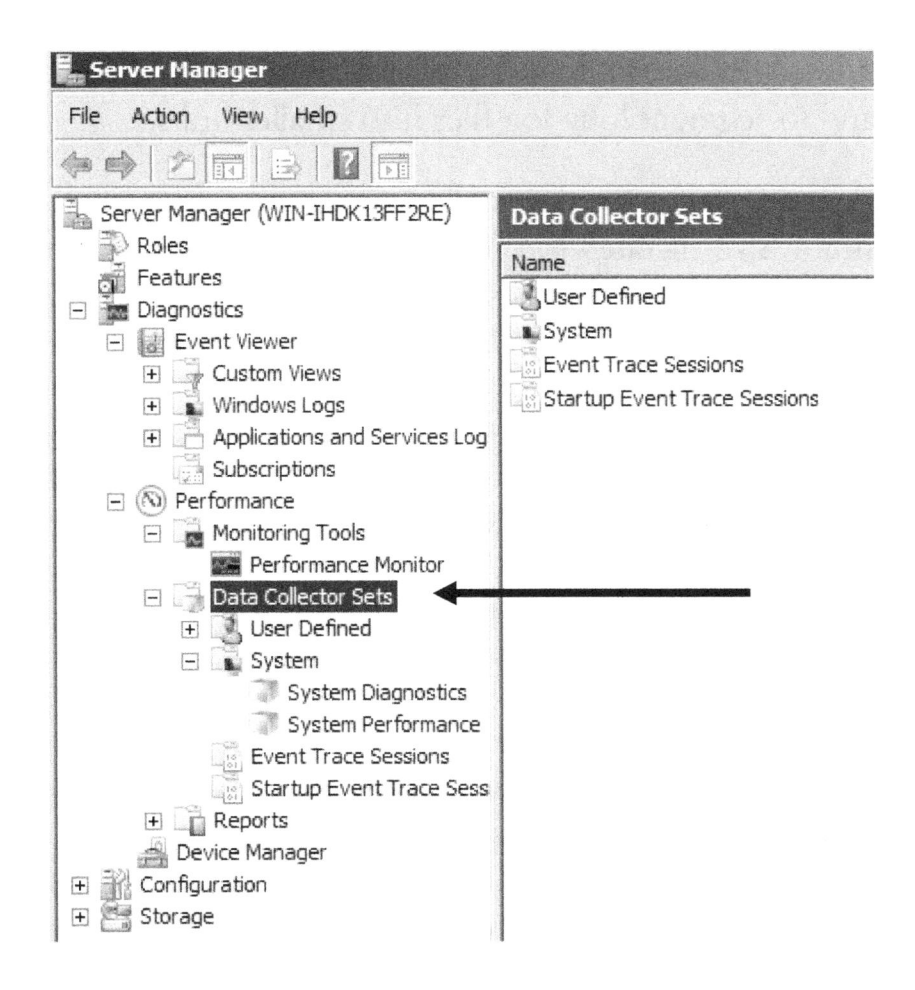

There are several important points you want to remember.

- In order to create a data collector set, you have to be logged on as a member of the local Administrators or Performance Log Users group.

- Data Collector Set creates log files. These log files are NOT backward-compatible with earlier versions of Windows. However, logs created by earlier versions of Windows can be viewed in Windows Server 2008 R2.

- The Data Manager function handles the management of log data.

- Large log files often result in longer report generation times. You may use the relog command to segment long log files into smaller units.

- Duration refers to the time period for data collection to write to a single log file, while Maximum Size dictates the restarting or stopping of the Data Collector Set when the log file reaches its size limit. An expiration date for a collector is not intended for stopping data collection in progress on that date. It is only for preventing new instances of data collection from starting after the expiration date.

- Resource policy determines whether to delete the oldest or largest log file or directory when the respective size limits are reached. Maximum root path size specifies the max size of the data directory used by the Data Collector Set. Concern on log size becomes important for busy computers in a busy network!

- A Windows Server system can slow down significantly when a single process is using too much processor time, that an application is utilizing the processor fully, or that an application is running in a loop or simply not responding. You need to identify which process is associated with the problematic application and then act accordingly.

## Resource Monitoring

Resource Monitor provides real time information on CPU, disk, network, and memory usage. You have to be a member of the local Administrators group or equivalent in order to use Resource Monitor. If you see constantly high utilization in a particular area, further investigation may be necessary.

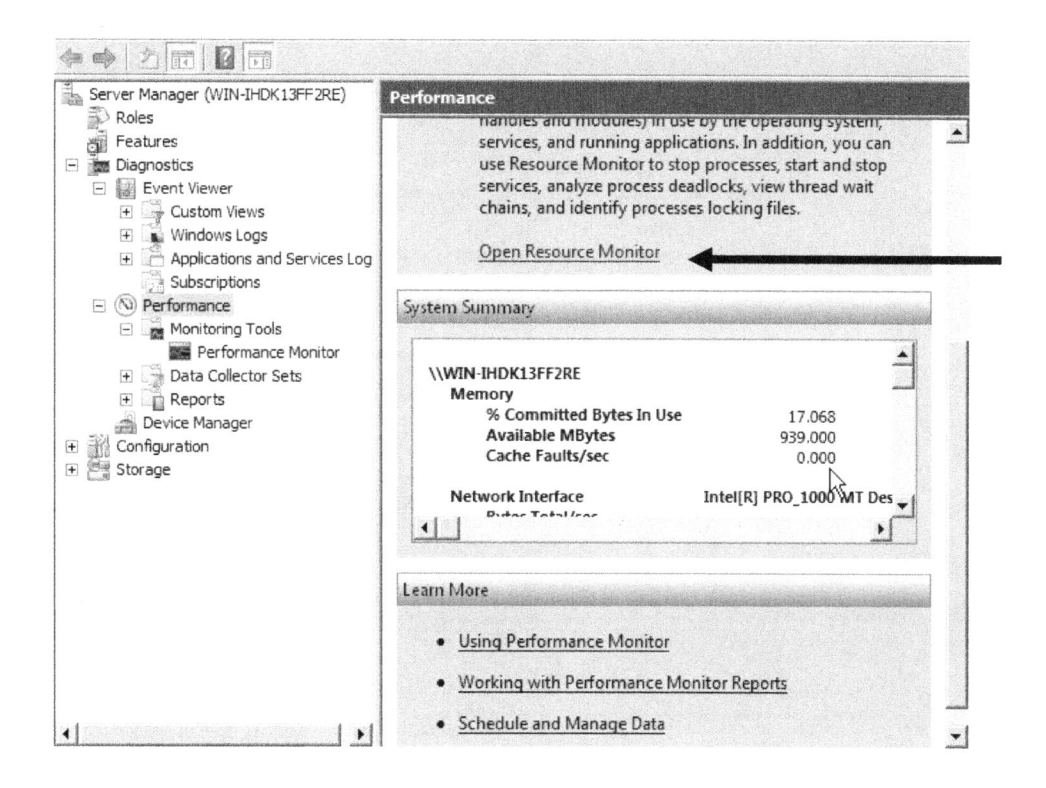

You can actually use Resource Monitor to monitor I/O performance at the file level. Information on reads, writes, and response time for individual files are all available. You want to know that Response Time in milliseconds should be kept low - anything less than 10 ms is considered good.

## Power Options

The Power Plan is all about energy conservation. Through Control Panel or powercfg.cpl via the command line you can invoke the interface which lets you choose a power plan. The default plan is Balanced, which should be ok for most scenarios.

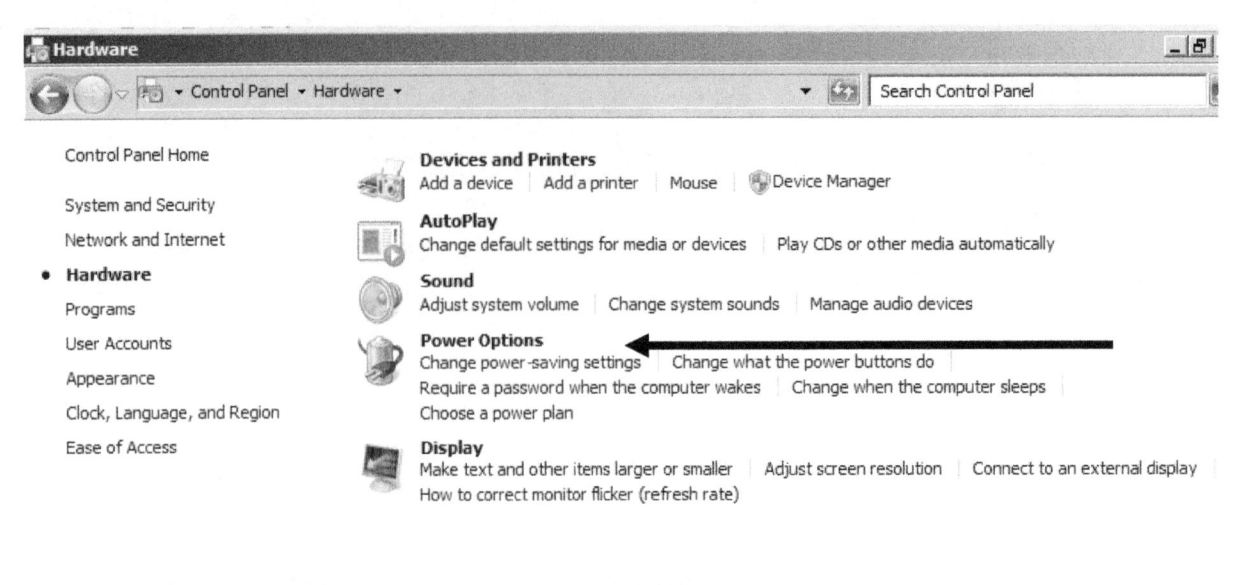

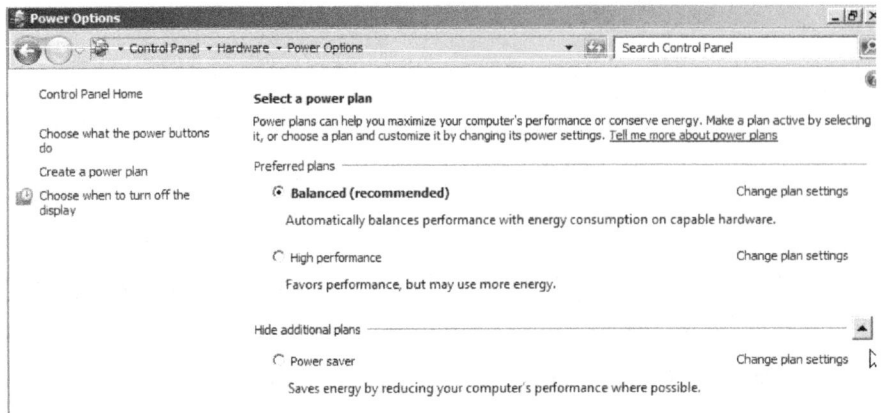

You want to know that Windows Server 2008 R2 does not have built-in support for UPS device. You must use the manufacturer's driver for installation purpose.

## Volume Shadow Copy Service

VSS aims to create a consistent shadow copy (which is a snapshot/point-in-time copy) of the data to be backed up. The VSS service ensures that all VSS components can communicate with each other properly. The VSS requester requests the actual creation of shadow copies through a backup application. The VSS writer ensures there is a consistent data set to back up. The VSS provider creates and maintains the shadow copies via either software or hardware.

Complete copy means making a complete full and read-only copy of the original volume at a given point in time. Copy-on-write makes a differential copy by copying changes only. Redirect-on-write does not make any changes to the original volume but makes a differential copy through redirecting changes to a different volume. In terms of compatibility, note that a transportable shadow copy created on Windows Server 2003 cannot be imported onto a server running Windows Server 2008 or 2008 R2. A transportable shadow copy created on Windows Server 2008 or 2008 R2 cannot be imported onto a server running Server 2003. A shadow copy created on Windows Server 2008, however, can be imported onto a server running 2008 R2 without any problem. Note that in the case of hard disk drive backup, the shadow copy created is the same as a backup - you can have data copied off the shadow copy for a restore, or you can use the shadow copy for a fast recovery.

## Review Questions:

1. Event logging starts automatically when you start Windows Server. True?

2. Only administrators can view the security logs. True?

3. Application or program events are classified into error, warning, and ...

4. Compare warning with error.

5. What are security-related events?

6. Setup event log file has the name of:

7. Events logged are saved in what format?

8. You can access perfmon via which command?

9. Log files are backward-compatible with Windows XP. True?

10. Large log files often result in:

11. Long log files can be segmented through which command?

12. Resource policy determines:

13. Maximum root path size determines:

14. Resource Monitor provides real time information on:

15. What is a power plan? How do you configure one?

16. What is the purpose of VSS?

17. In the context of VSS, compare Complete copy with Copy-on-write.

## Answers:

1. *Event logging starts automatically when you start Windows Server.*

2. *Only administrators can view the security logs.*

3. *Application or program events are classified into error, warning, and information depending on their seriousness.*

4. *An error describes a significant problem. A warning is not yet a significant problem but is likely a problem soon.*

5. *Security-related events are audits that describe success or failure of an event.*

6. *The log file is called Setup.etl.*

7. *Events logged are saved in XML format.*

8. *You can access perfmon via the perfmon.msc (or perfmon.exe through the command line).*

9. *Log files are NOT backward-compatible with Windows XP.*

10. *Large log files often result in longer report generation times.*

11. *You may use the relog command to segment long log files into smaller units.*

12. *Resource policy determines whether to delete the oldest or largest log file or directory when the respective size limits are reached.*

13. *Maximum root path size specifies the max size of the data directory used by the Data Collector Set.*

14. *Resource Monitor provides real time information on CPU, disk, network, and memory usage.*

15. *The Power Plan is all about energy conservation. Through Control Panel or powercfg.cpl via the command line you can invoke the interface which lets you choose a power plan.*

16. *VSS aims to create a consistent shadow copy (which is a snapshot/point-in-time copy) of the data to be backed up.*

17. *Complete copy means making a complete full and read-only copy of the original volume at a given point in time. Copy-on-write makes a differential copy by copying changes only.*

# User Management and Backup & Recovery

**Shared Folders**

You can create folder share simply by right clicking on the folder and choose the appropriate sharing option. You can also manage shared folders via Computer Management. The Shares node shows all shared folders on the computer while the Sessions node displays full details on which remote users currently are connected to the shared folders. You can easily edit the properties of a share by right-clicking it and then select properties. You can also create a shared folder by right-clicking the Shares node and then choose New Share for invoking the Create a Shared Folder Wizard.

An alternative to using the GUI is to use the net share command. You can use net share to create, configure and delete network shares from the command line. The /grant switch specifies the access rights granted, while /users specifies the max number of users who can access the share. As a user of a shared resource, one can use net use to connect to or disconnect from a shared resource, or displays information about the available computer connections. Resource must be specified in this format - \\ ComputerName \ ShareName. You can use /user to specify a different user name with which the connection is being made. You can also use /savecred to store the provided credentials for easy reuse.

**Users and Groups**

Local users and groups can be managed through the Server Manager. You can create, modify or remove users and groups as needed.

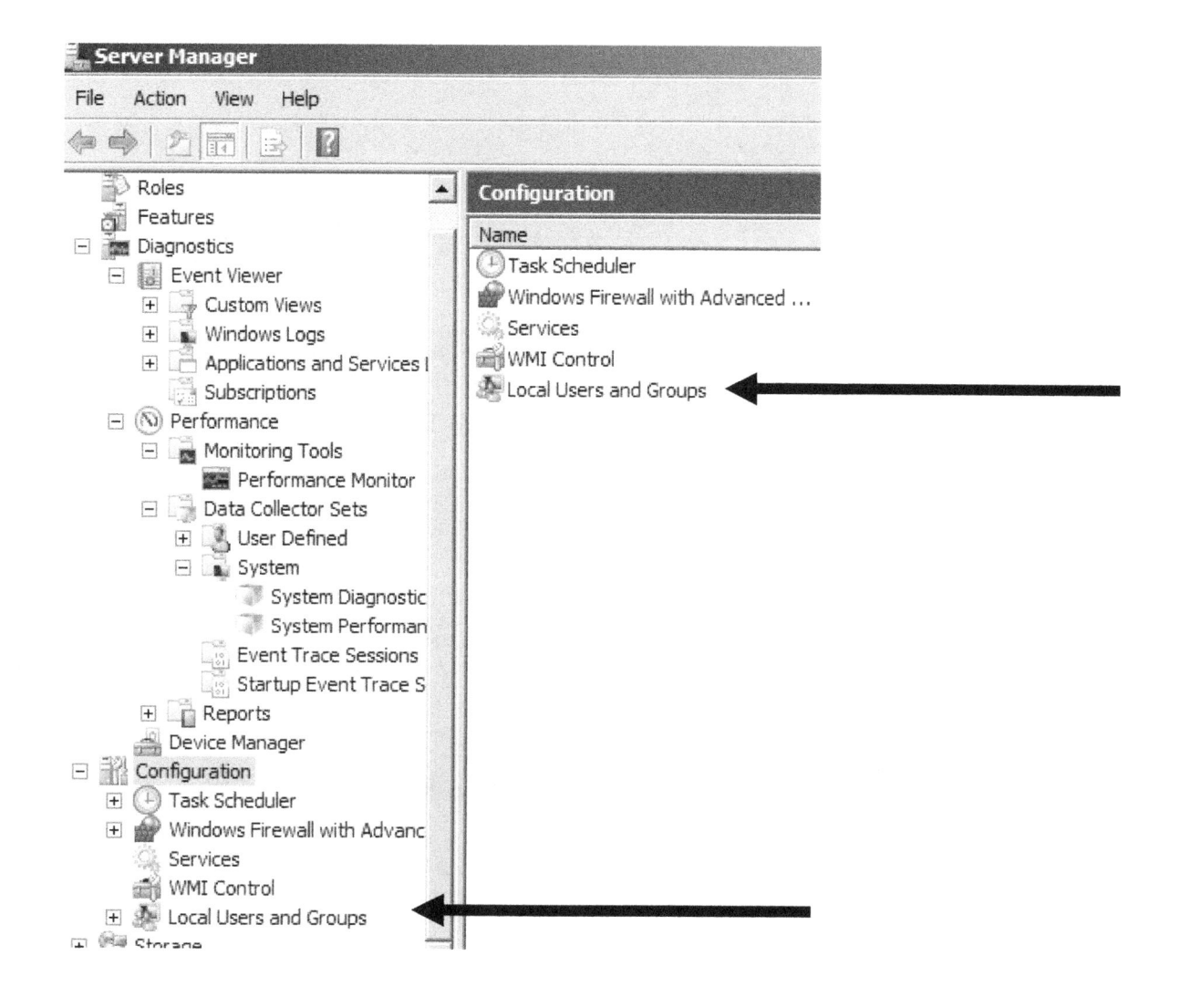

The two default user accounts are Administrator and Guest. A bunch of default groups are also in there. The Administrator account cannot be deleted. You also cannot have it removed from the Administrators group. However, you may have it renamed or disabled. Renaming it to something else can make hacking more difficult. Do keep in mind, even when the Administrator account is disabled, it can still be used for access through Safe Mode. In fact one can use the System Configuration tool (msconfig) to restart in Safe Mode. One can also boot into Safe Mode by pressing the **"F8"** key just before the Windows boot screen appears.

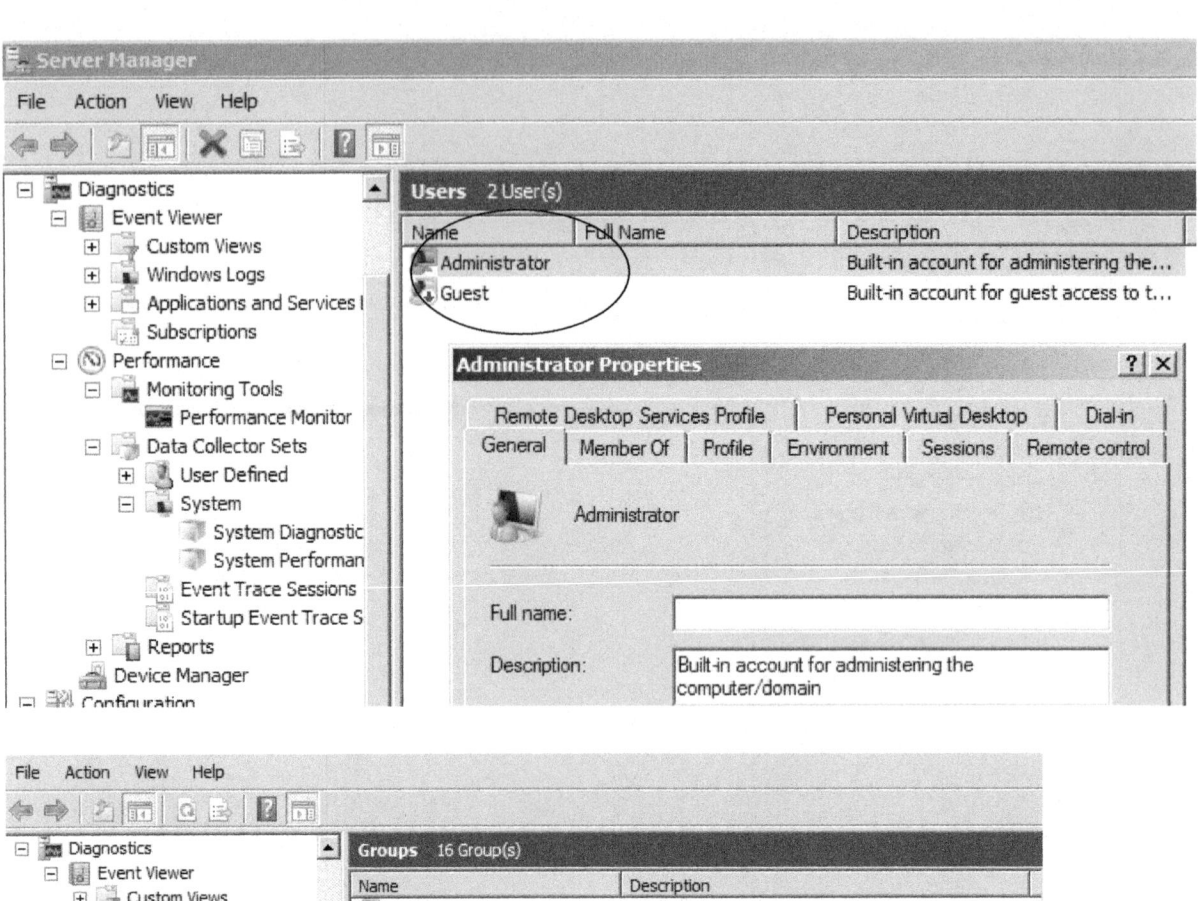

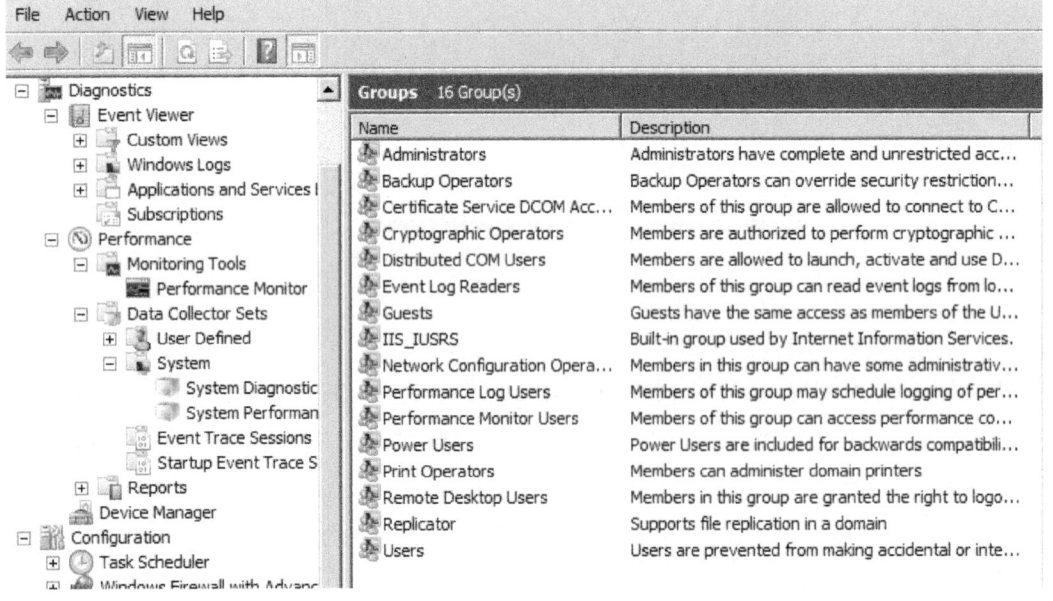

The Groups folder shows the default local groups as well as the local groups that you have created. You should limit the number of users in the

Administrators group since these people have Full Control permissions on the local computer. Unless strictly necessary, you should leave the Guest account disabled. This Guest account is dangerous since it does not require a password, but it is disabled by default anyway. Do note that some default user rights that are assigned to certain default local groups may actually allow members of those groups to exercise additional admin rights on the local computer, so you should equally trust all personnel that are members of the Administrators and Backup Operators groups.

IIS_IUSRS is a built-in group used only by IIS. Network Configuration Operators can make changes to TCP/IP settings. Performance Log Users can manage performance counters, logs, and alerts locally and from remote clients. Performance Monitor Users can monitor performance counters locally and from remote clients.

Power Users is a legacy feature. Remote Desktop Users can log on to the computer remotely. Replicator is for logging onto the Replicator services of a domain controller and should not be used to accommodate user accounts of actual users. Backup Operators can back up and restore files regardless of any permission that protect those files but they cannot change any of the related security settings.

**Local users are NOT the same as domain users. Domain users have their accounts stored in AD, not just locally. Domain admins can perform tasks that involved AD. Local admins can only perform admin tasks on the local machine.**

# Backup

From within Server Manager you can invoke the Server Backup console and its wizard for creating backups. You can use it to back up a full server (which means all volumes), selected volumes, or the system state. You can later recover volumes, folders, files, certain applications, or the system state. You can create and manage backups for the local computer or a remote computer. However, since this MMC console snap-in is not available for the Server Core installation option, to run backups for Server Core installations you need to either use the command line or perform backups remotely from another computer.

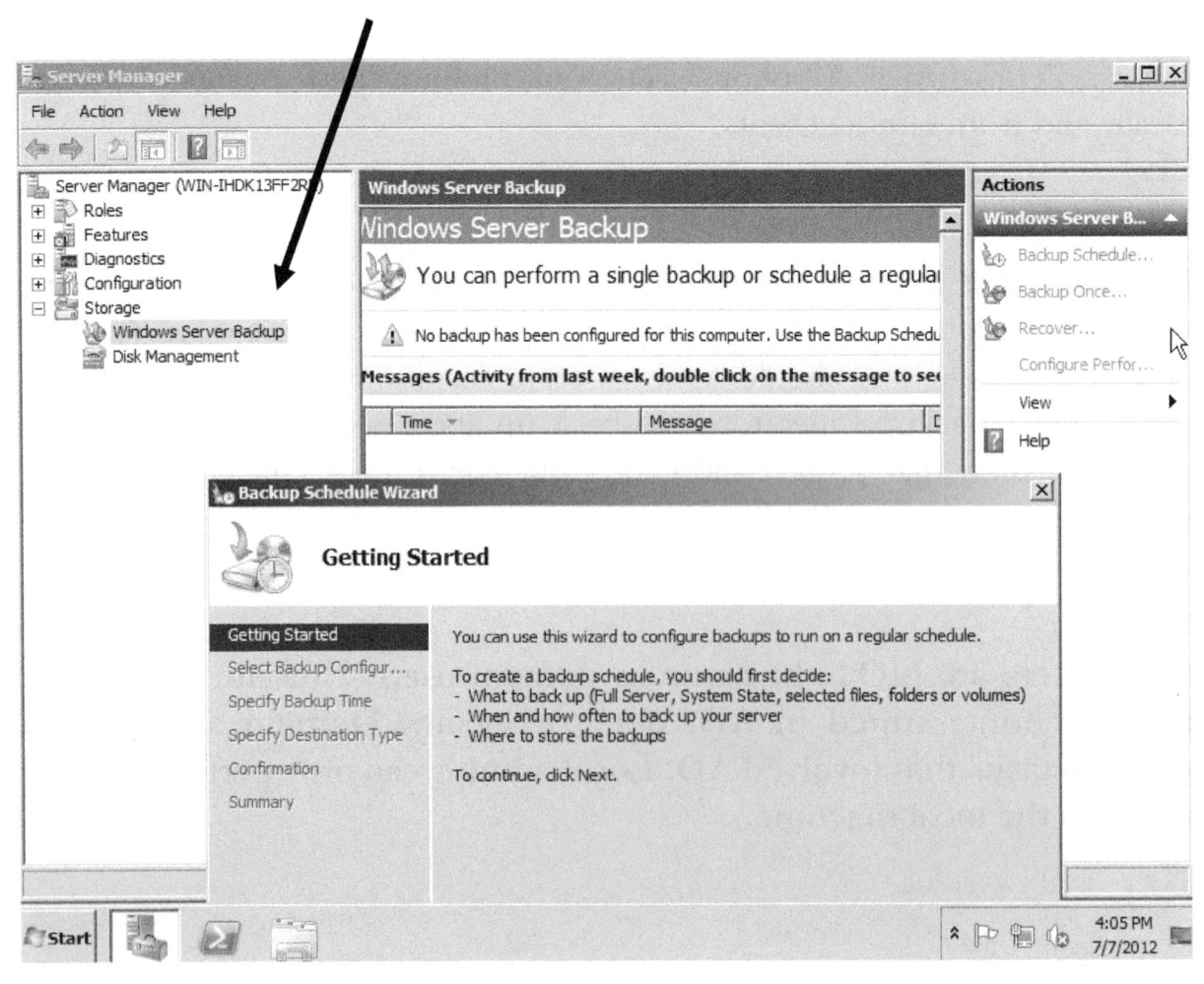

## Backup Schedule Wizard

### Select Backup Configuration

- Getting Started
- **Select Backup Configur...**
- Specify Backup Time
- Specify Destination Type
- Confirmation
- Summary

What type of configuration do you want to schedule?

- ● Full server (recommended)
  I want to back up all my server data, applications and system state.
  Backup size: 8.28 GB

- ○ Custom
  I want to choose custom volumes, files for backup.

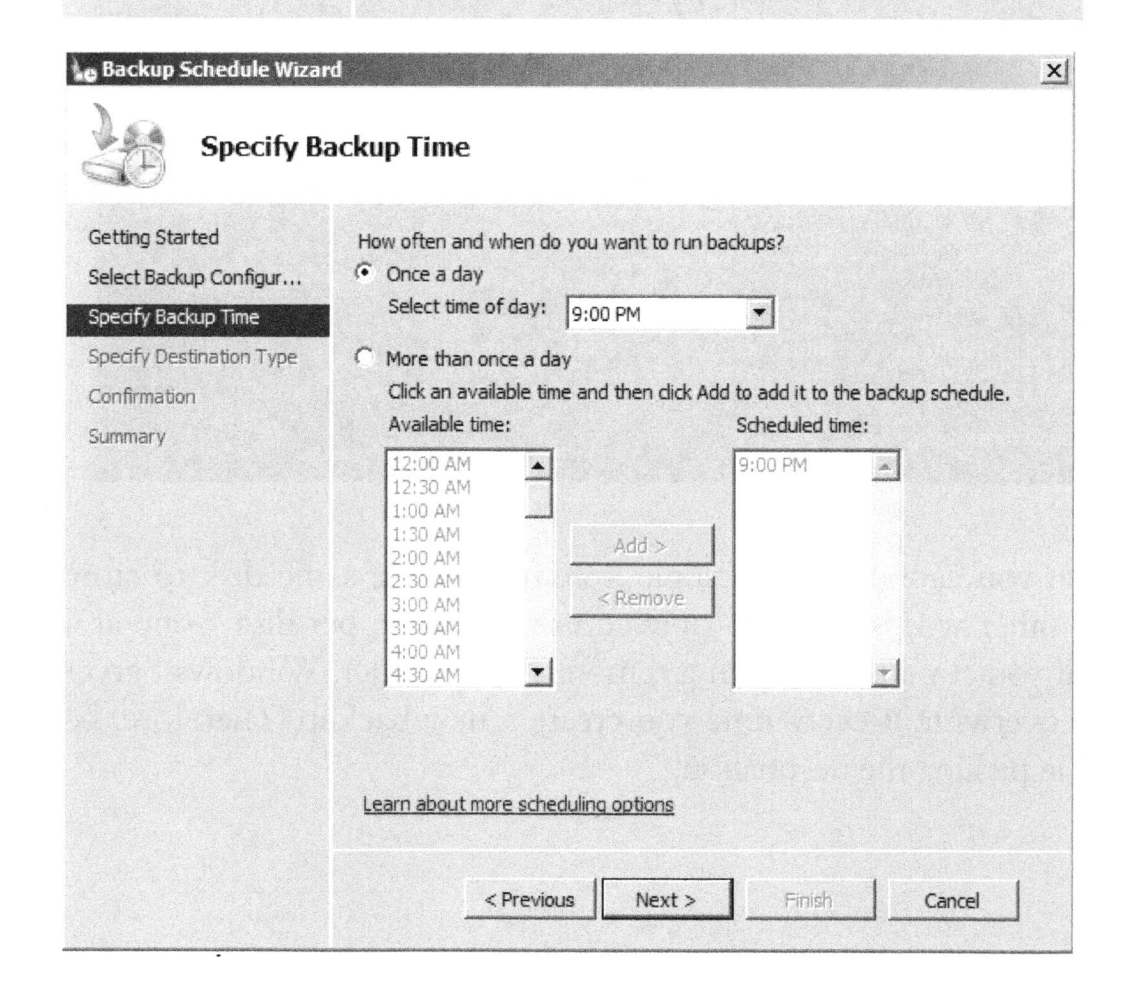

---

## Backup Schedule Wizard

### Specify Backup Time

- Getting Started
- Select Backup Configur...
- **Specify Backup Time**
- Specify Destination Type
- Confirmation
- Summary

How often and when do you want to run backups?

- ● Once a day
  Select time of day: 9:00 PM

- ○ More than once a day
  Click an available time and then click Add to add it to the backup schedule.

  Available time:
  - 12:00 AM
  - 12:30 AM
  - 1:00 AM
  - 1:30 AM
  - 2:00 AM
  - 2:30 AM
  - 3:00 AM
  - 3:30 AM
  - 4:00 AM
  - 4:30 AM

  Scheduled time:
  - 9:00 PM

  [ Add > ]  [ < Remove ]

Learn about more scheduling options

[ < Previous ]  [ Next > ]  [ Finish ]  [ Cancel ]

In Windows Server 2008 R2 you may use the Windows Server Backup MMC snap-in, the Wbadmin command, or the Windows PowerShell cmdlets to make backups. You may only use the Windows Server Backup MMC snap-in or the Wbadmin command for performing recovery operations.

```
C:\Users\Administrator>wbadmin
wbadmin 1.0 - Backup command-line tool
(C) Copyright 2004 Microsoft Corp.

ERROR - Command incomplete. See the list below.
For Help for this command, type WBADMIN <command> /?.

---- Commands Supported ----
ENABLE BACKUP              -- Creates or modifies a daily backup schedule.
DISABLE BACKUP             -- Disables the scheduled backups.
START BACKUP               -- Runs a one-time backup.
STOP JOB                   -- Stops the currently running backup or recovery
                              operation.
GET VERSIONS               -- List details of backups recoverable from a
                              specified location.
GET ITEMS                  -- Lists items contained in a backup.
START RECOVERY             -- Runs a recovery.
GET STATUS                 -- Reports the status of the currently running
                              operation.
GET DISKS                  -- Lists the disks that are currently online.
START SYSTEMSTATERECOVERY  -- Runs a system state recovery.
START SYSTEMSTATEBACKUP    -- Runs a system state backup.
DELETE SYSTEMSTATEBACKUP   -- Deletes one or more system state backups.

C:\Users\Administrator>
```

Do note that you cannot pick multiple volumes on the same disk to store backups. In other words, you can only add one volume per disk - one at a time. Also, if you store a backup in a remote shared folder, Windows Server Backup will overwrite it every time you create a new backup. Therefore, be very careful in picking the destination!

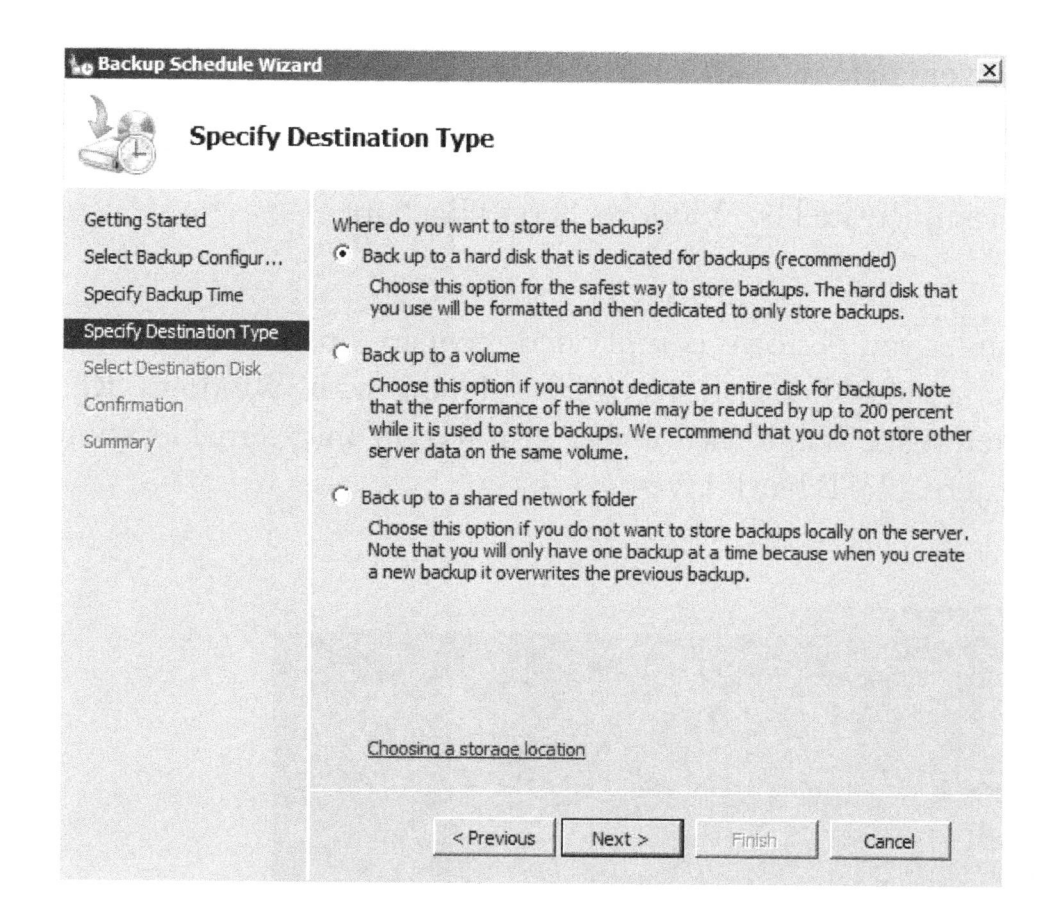

## Recovery options

The Windows recovery environment WinRE serves as a reference base against unwanted changes that might be made by software. The source image for WinRE includes drivers and files separately maintained from the main Windows installation so it will not be affected by any software changes. **Windows Setup will install Windows RE by default. That is,** Windows RE is preloaded onto every Windows Server 2008 R2 installation except for the Server Core installation. The default Windows RE image known as Winre.wim is placed in the OS partition when Install.wim is being applied to disk. All the required Windows RE configurations are automatically set after OOBE. To manually enter Windows RE, boot using a Windows setup disc or restart the server system, then press F8 immediately after the POST process. Choose Repair Your Computer. Do remember that Windows RE provides you with the System Image Recovery option, allowing you to restore from a backup created by Windows Server Backup.

Windows RE can let you perform complicated recovery operation. You can actually integrate a non-Microsoft recovery solution with Windows RE, provided that a reference Windows 7 image is stored on an external location (most likely an external USB hard drive).

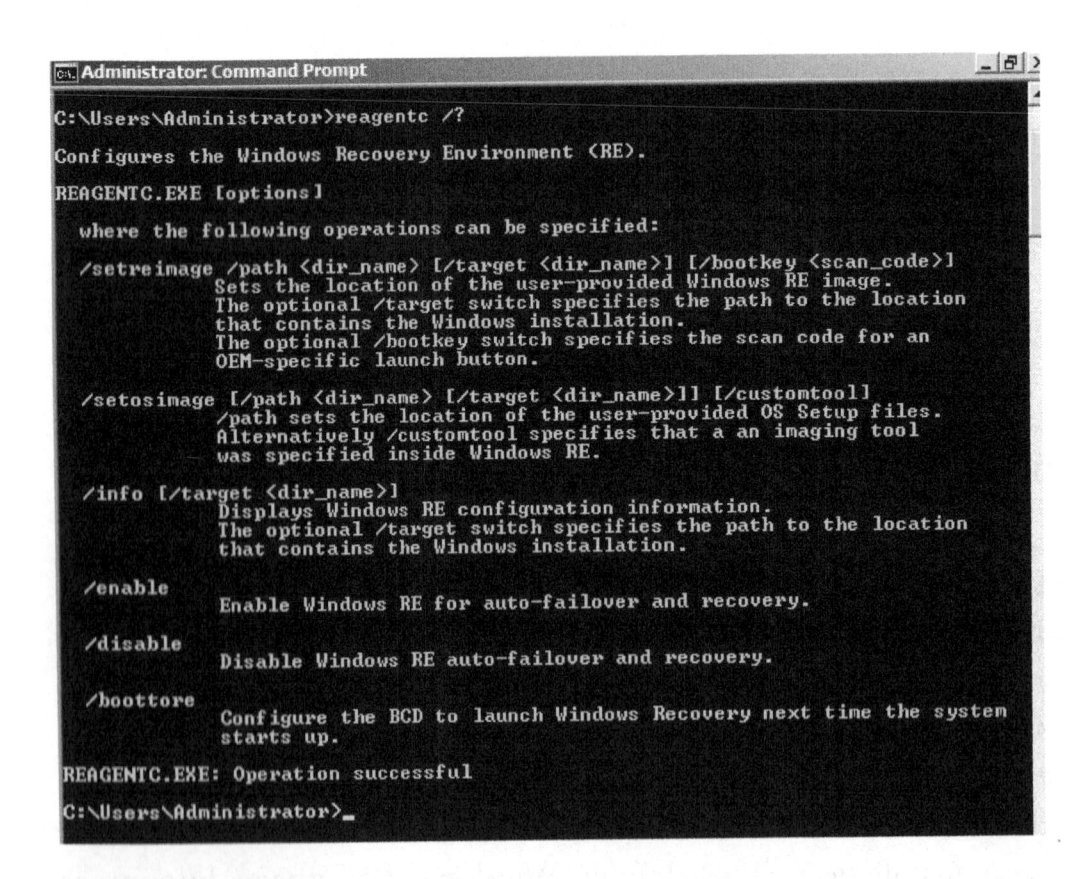

```
C:\Users\Administrator>reagentc /?
Configures the Windows Recovery Environment (RE).
REAGENTC.EXE [options]
    where the following operations can be specified:

    /setreimage /path <dir_name> [/target <dir_name>] [/bootkey <scan_code>]
                Sets the location of the user-provided Windows RE image.
                The optional /target switch specifies the path to the location
                that contains the Windows installation.
                The optional /bootkey switch specifies the scan code for an
                OEM-specific launch button.

    /setosimage [/path <dir_name> [/target <dir_name>]] [/customtool]
                /path sets the location of the user-provided OS Setup files.
                Alternatively /customtool specifies that a an imaging tool
                was specified inside Windows RE.

    /info [/target <dir_name>]
                Displays Windows RE configuration information.
                The optional /target switch specifies the path to the location
                that contains the Windows installation.

    /enable
                Enable Windows RE for auto-failover and recovery.

    /disable
                Disable Windows RE auto-failover and recovery.

    /boottore
                Configure the BCD to launch Windows Recovery next time the system
                starts up.
REAGENTC.EXE: Operation successful

C:\Users\Administrator>_
```

You use Reagentc at the command line to manage Windows RE. The /setreimage option can be used to set the source location of the custom Windows RE image, while /bootkey can be used to specify the scan code of a custom hardware key for starting Windows RE. /enable is an option for configuring the required BCD and other settings to start Windows RE. /disable is for removing all Windows RE settings. With /boottore you can explicitly specify that the next time the system starts up, Windows RE will get started automatically. /info is for revealing the current status of Windows RE.

**The BCD registry file actually replaces the Boot.ini files.** Msconfig.exe is a troubleshooting tool for configuring various startup options. BCDEdit.exe replaces Bootcfg.exe in Windows XP - you can run it at an administrative command prompt. The BCD Windows Management Instrumentation provider serves as a management interface for scripting utilities that modify BCD.

```
C:\Users\Administrator>bcdedit

Windows Boot Manager
--------------------
identifier              {bootmgr}
device                  partition=\Device\HarddiskVolume1
description             Windows Boot Manager
locale                  en-US
inherit                 {globalsettings}
default                 {current}
resumeobject            {85af69fe-c83e-11e1-8538-b36f854f19b4}
displayorder            {current}
toolsdisplayorder       {memdiag}
timeout                 30

Windows Boot Loader
-------------------
identifier              {current}
device                  partition=C:
path                    \Windows\system32\winload.exe
description             Windows Server 2008 R2
locale                  en-US
inherit                 {bootloadersettings}
recoverysequence        {85af6a00-c83e-11e1-8538-b36f854f19b4}
recoveryenabled         Yes
osdevice                partition=C:
systemroot              \Windows
resumeobject            {85af69fe-c83e-11e1-8538-b36f854f19b4}
nx                      OptOut

C:\Users\Administrator>_
```

BCDEdit is a tool you can use to change the default boot settings on a multiboot computer. You can use it to adjust the timeout and change the descriptions of the various boot menu items. Technically it replaces the settings in the older boot.ini found in Windows 2000 and XP.

## Safe Mode and Last Known Good Configuration

If Windows Server fails suddenly, next time you start up you will see the recovery option screen and you may choose to boot through safe mode or use last known good configuration:

```
                        Windows Error Recovery
Windows failed to start. A recent hardware or software change might be the
cause. To fix the problem:

   1. Insert your Windows installation disc and restart your computer.
   2. Choose your language settings, and then click "Next."
   3. Click "Repair your computer."

Other options:
If power was interrupted during startup, choose Start Windows Normally.
(Use the arrow keys to highlight your choice.)

      Safe Mode
      Safe Mode with Networking
      Safe Mode with Command Prompt
      Last Known Good Configuration (advanced)
      Start Windows Normally

Seconds until the highlighted choice will be selected automatically: 26
Description: Start Windows with its regular settings.
```

Last Known Good Configuration enables you to load the last working version of Windows Server. Safe Mode gives access to basic files and drivers. Safe Mode with Networking loads all these drivers plus the essential services and drivers to enable networking. Safe mode aims to help you diagnose problems. Last known good configuration attempts to help you get back to work ASAP.

## Questions:

1. What are the two default user accounts?

2. The Administrator account cannot be deleted. However, you can have it removed from the Administrators group. True?

3. _____ is a built-in group used only by IIS.

4. Describe the Replicator group.

5. Describe the Backup Operators group.

6. From where can you invoke the Server Backup console?

7. How do you run backups for Server Core installations?

8. In Windows Server 2008 R2 you may make backups via what tools?

9. What is Msconfig.exe for?

10. BCDEdit.exe replaces:

11. You may use _____ at the command line to manage Windows RE.

12. Compare Last Known Good Configuration with Safe Mode.

# Answers:

1. The two default user accounts are Administrator and Guest.

2. The Administrator account cannot be deleted. You also cannot have it removed from the Administrators group. However, you may have it renamed or disabled.

3. IIS_IUSRS is a built-in group used only by IIS.

4. Replicator is for logging onto the Replicator services of a domain controller and should not be used to accommodate user accounts of actual users.

5. Backup Operators can back up and restore files regardless of any permission that protect those files but they cannot change any of the related security settings.

6. From within Server Manager you can invoke the Server Backup console and its wizard for creating backups.

7. To run backups for Server Core installations you need to either use the command line or perform backups remotely from another computer.

8. In Windows Server 2008 R2 you may use the Windows Server Backup MMC snap-in, the Wbadmin command, or the Windows PowerShell cmdlets to make backups.

9. Msconfig.exe is a troubleshooting tool for configuring various startup options.

10. BCDEdit.exe replaces Bootcfg.exe.

11. You use Reagentc at the command line to manage Windows RE.

12. Last Known Good Configuration enables you to load the last working version of Windows Server. Safe Mode gives access to basic files and drivers.

# Setting up Active Directory

## Basic concepts of AD

Active Directory AD stores information of all network objects and makes the information easy to find. It is a logical and hierarchical presentation and storage of shared resources such as servers, volumes, printers...etc. A global catalog is a domain controller. Every AD has at least one. It stores a copy of all Active Directory objects in a forest. To be precise, it stores a full copy of all objects in the directory for its own domain and a partial copy of all objects for all other domains.

It enables and facilitates user searches for directory information throughout all domains. It also resolves user principal names when the authenticating domain controller doesn't have knowledge of the involved account. And it helps other domain controllers to validate references to those objects that belong to other domains in the forest. The role it plays is very important in the authentication process. If it is not available when a user logs on to a domain, the computer will try to use the cached credentials to log on the user. However, if the user has not logged on before, he will only be able to log on to the local computer.

## Installing a domain controller and changing the functional level

You need to install the Active Directory Domain Services AD-DS role on the server so to allow the server to act as a Domain Controller. After this you need to use the dcpromo command to invoke the AD Installation Wizard. If you use the /adv switch you can run the wizard in advanced mode. To perform all the setup tasks, you should be a local admin as well as a domain admin. And you should also have a special restore mode admin password. You will be asked to setup separate password for restore use later.

**Add Roles Wizard**

## Select Server Roles

Before You Begin
**Server Roles**
Active Directory Domain Services
Confirmation
Progress
Results

Select one or more roles to install on this server.

Roles:

- [ ] Active Directory Certificate Services
- [x] **Active Directory Domain Services**  ←
- [ ] Active Directory Federation Services
- [ ] Active Directory Lightweight Directory Services
- [ ] Active Directory Rights Management Services
- [ ] Application Server
- [ ] DHCP Server
- [ ] DNS Server
- [ ] Fax Server

---

The following roles, role services, or features were installed successfully:

⚠ 1 warning, 1 informational messages below

⚠ Windows automatic updating is not enabled. To install the latest updates, use Windows Update in Control Panel to check for updates.

⌃ **Active Directory Domain Services**          ✅ **Installation succeeded**

The following role services were installed:
**Active Directory Domain Controller**
ⓘ Use the Active Directory Domain Services Installation Wizard (dcpromo.exe) to make the server a fully functional domain controller.
Close this wizard and launch the Active Directory Domain Services Installation Wizard (dcpromo.exe).

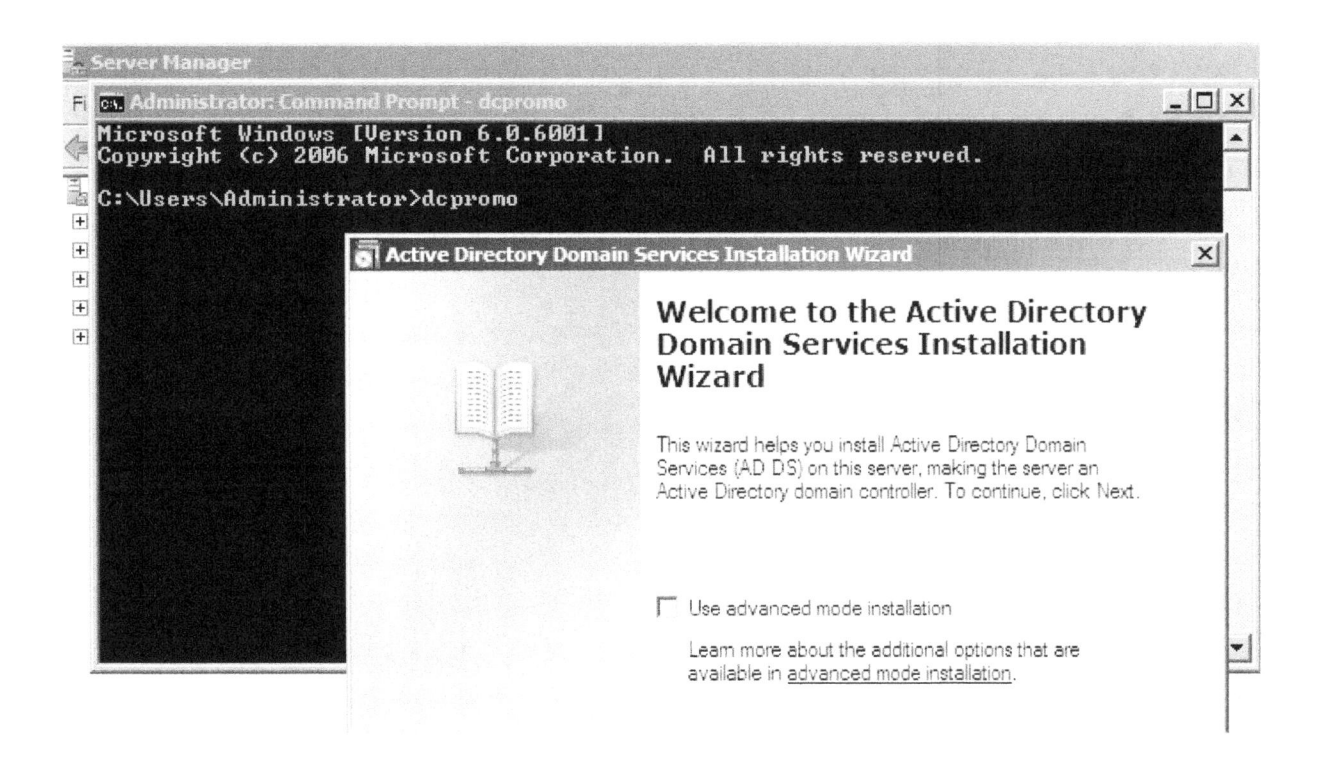

You need to have an NTFS partition with enough free space to hold the AD database files including the Active Directory database, the log files, and the SYSVOL shared folder. These are considered as System State data. For a simple installation with a single hard disk, you may accept the default directories. If you have multiple disks, you want to consider how you may backup the data. Keep in mind, you cannot backup data onto the same disk!

You need a properly functioning network card with proper IP addressing defined. Very importantly, you should use static IP address on this server. DHCP is not recommended. You also need to have an operational DNS server and a domain name for your organization. Without an existing DNS you will need to setup DNS on this same server.

Dcpromo will call up the wizard. You can choose to either join an existing forest or create a new forest. For demonstration purpose we create a new forest here. As the first server it must also act as a global catalog server. DNS should also be installed here. If no existing DNS infrastructure is in place, delegation will not be initially possible.

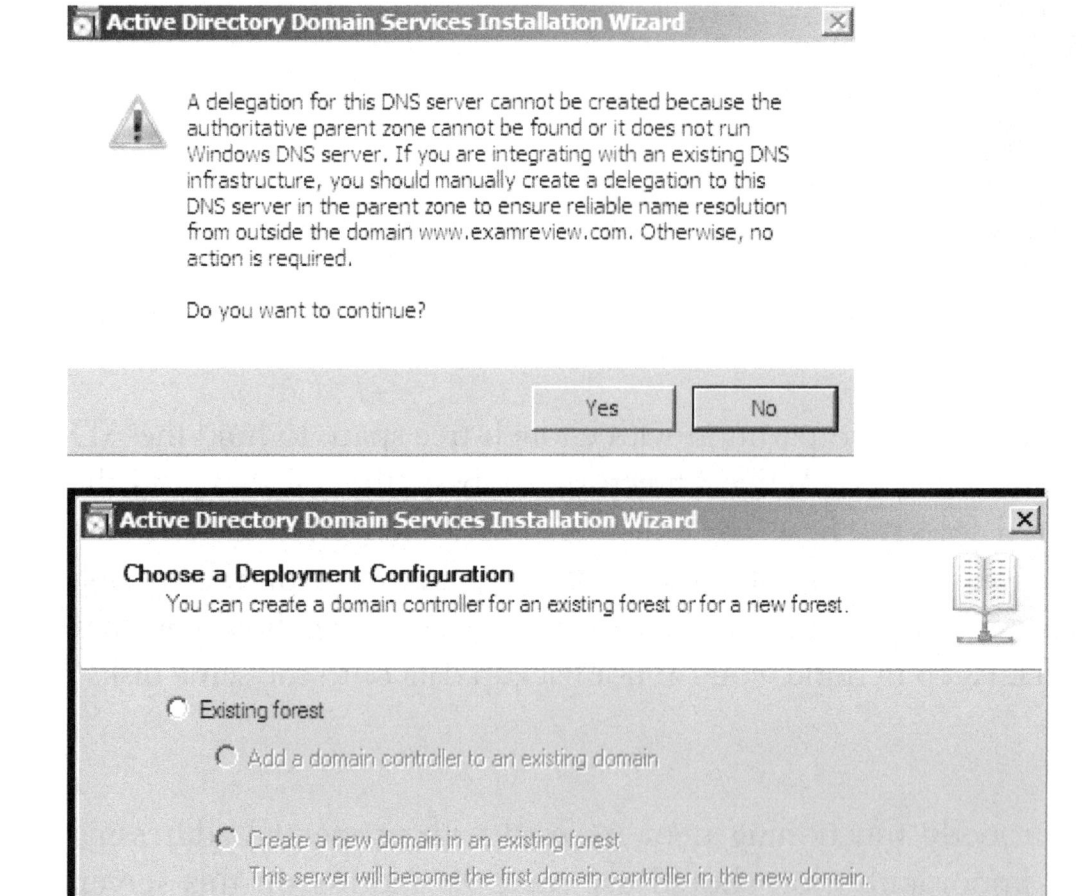

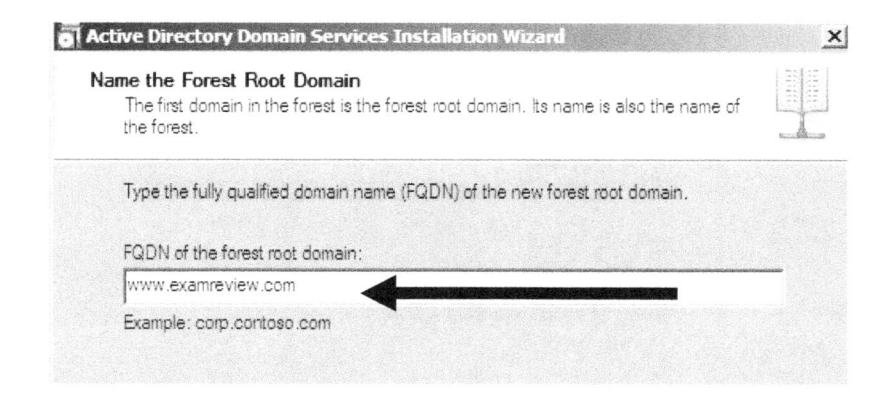

If you install a new Server 2008 R2 domain controller in an existing 2000 Server or Server 2003 based domain, and if this domain controller is also the first Windows Server 2008 R2 domain controller in the forest, you must prepare the forest by extending the schema via adprep. In Windows Server 2008 R2, Adprep.exe can be found in the /support/adprep folder of the DVD disc.

When the first Windows Server 2008–based Domain Controller is introduced, the forest will operate by default at the lowest functional level that is possible, which is Windows 2000, so that you may take advantage of the default Active Directory features while accommodating older versions of Windows Server. If you raise the functional level, newer advanced features can become available at the expense of compatibility. After you raise the domain functional level, domain controllers running earlier operating systems will not be able to participate in the domain. Ask yourself this question - is there a reason why older domain controllers should be retained? You need to be very careful because raising the domain functional levels to Windows Server 2008 is a task that can never be undone. In fact, all the existing Windows 2000–based or Windows Server 2003–based Domain Controllers will no longer function as expected.

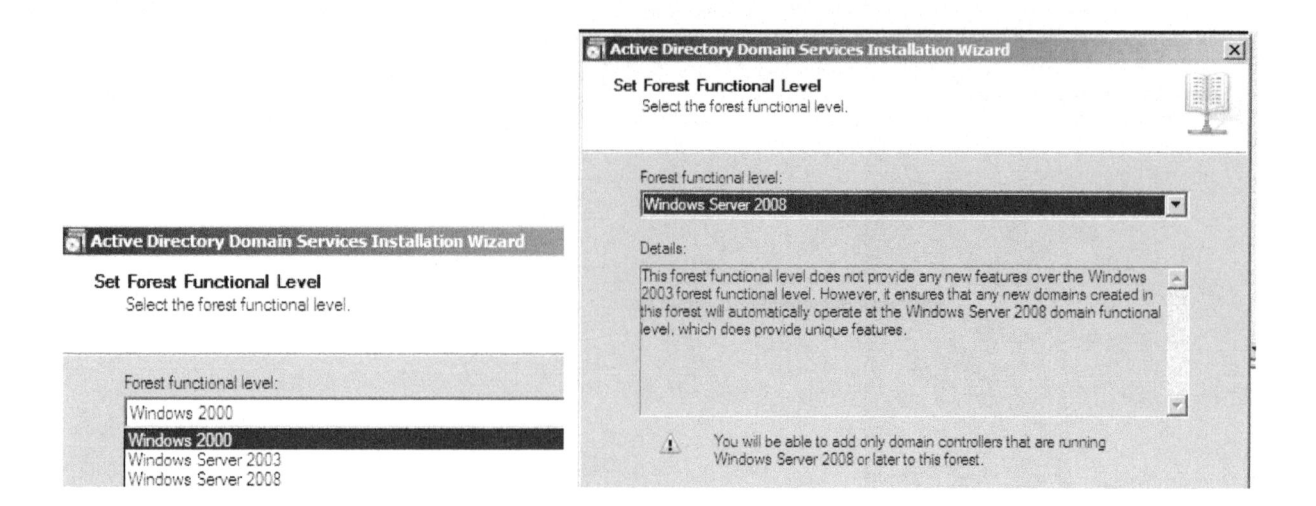

Do keep in mind, you can always raise the functional level later.

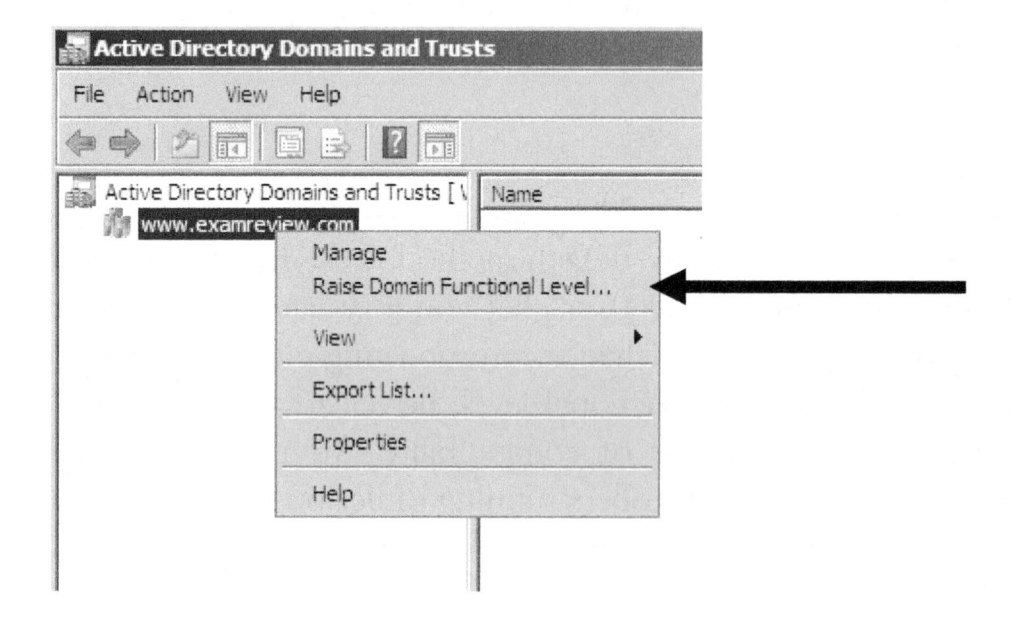

Along the installation process you will be asked to install DNS server. You will be suggested to use static IPs for the server as well.

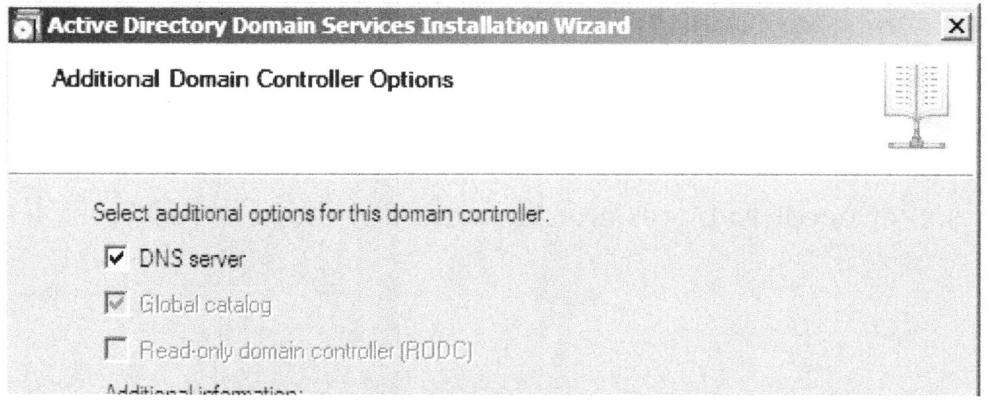

### Active Directory Domain Services Installation Wizard

**Additional Domain Controller Options**

Select additional options for this domain controller.

- ☑ DNS server
- ☑ Global catalog
- ☐ Read-only domain controller (RODC)

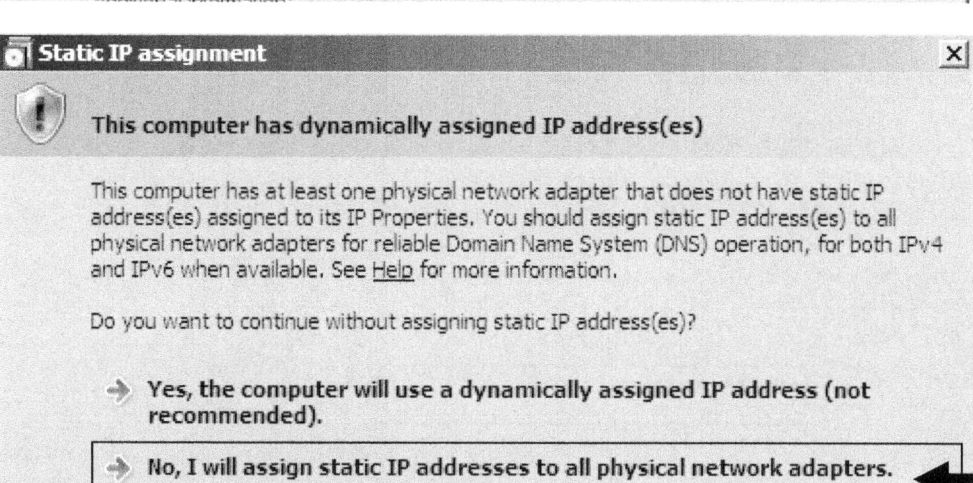

Additional information:

---

### Static IP assignment

**This computer has dynamically assigned IP address(es)**

This computer has at least one physical network adapter that does not have static IP address(es) assigned to its IP Properties. You should assign static IP address(es) to all physical network adapters for reliable Domain Name System (DNS) operation, for both IPv4 and IPv6 when available. See Help for more information.

Do you want to continue without assigning static IP address(es)?

→ Yes, the computer will use a dynamically assigned IP address (not recommended).

→ **No, I will assign static IP addresses to all physical network adapters.**

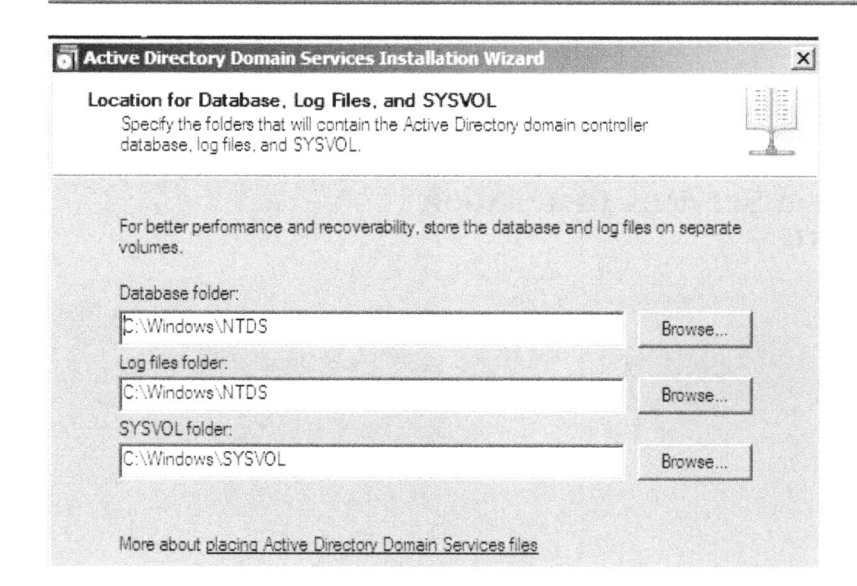

---

### Active Directory Domain Services Installation Wizard

**Location for Database, Log Files, and SYSVOL**
Specify the folders that will contain the Active Directory domain controller database, log files, and SYSVOL.

For better performance and recoverability, store the database and log files on separate volumes.

Database folder:
`C:\Windows\NTDS`    Browse...

Log files folder:
`C:\Windows\NTDS`    Browse...

SYSVOL folder:
`C:\Windows\SYSVOL`    Browse...

More about placing Active Directory Domain Services files

Directory Services Restore Mode DSRM is an alternate boot environment. With it your Windows Server can boot with the Active Directory database offline so you may perform routine maintenance as needed. Before you may boot into DSRM, the DSRM password must be set. After installation is completed, the server needs to be restarted in order for the new AD consoles to show up.

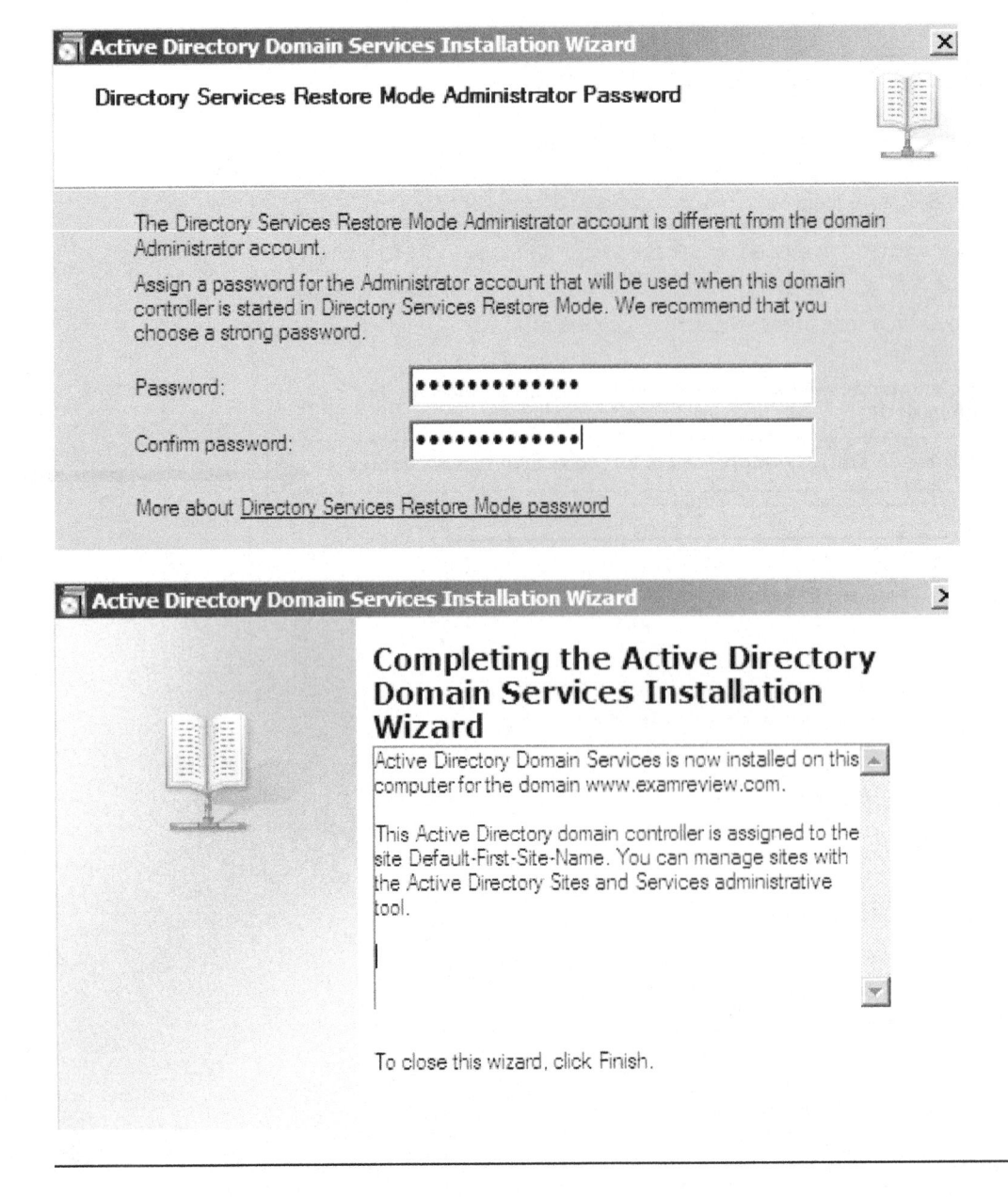

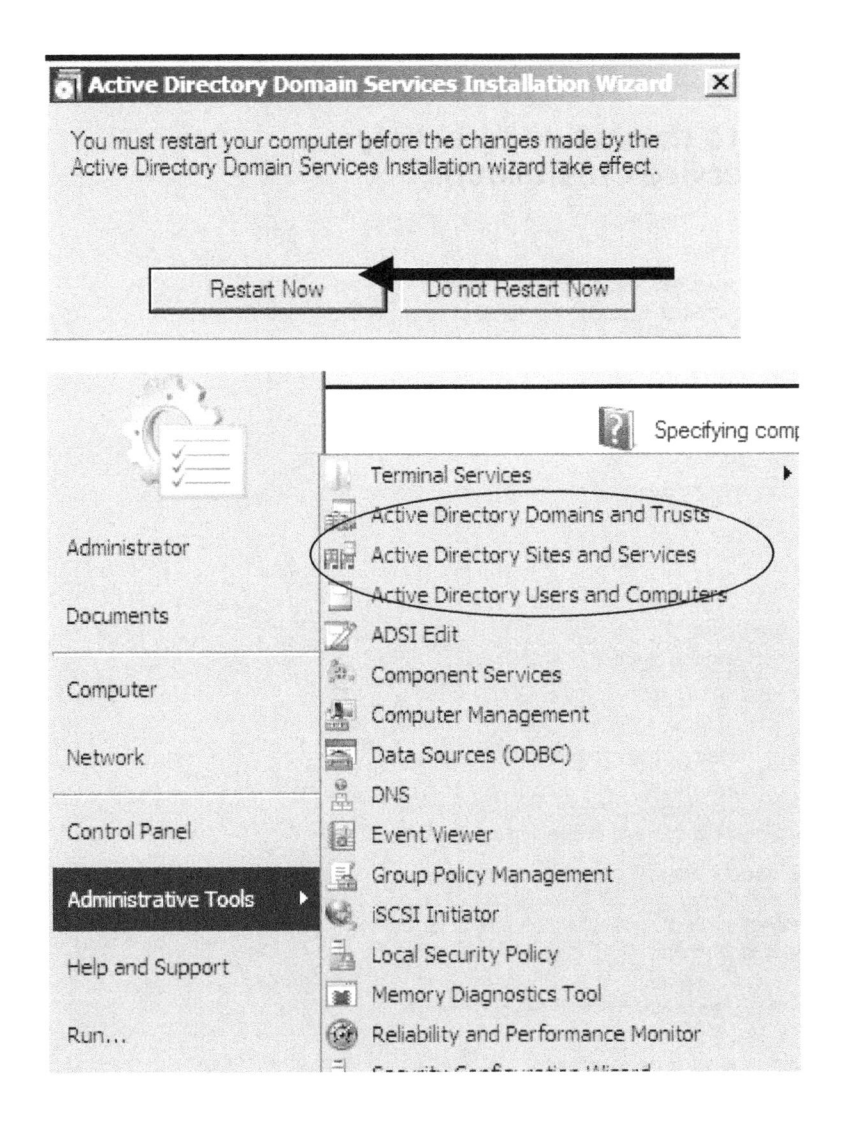

You may use Nltest.exe at the command line to show information on the Active Directory Domain Services. In the future, if you want to remove AD from the server, simply use DCPROMO to call up the wizard again. You will be able to delete AD from there.

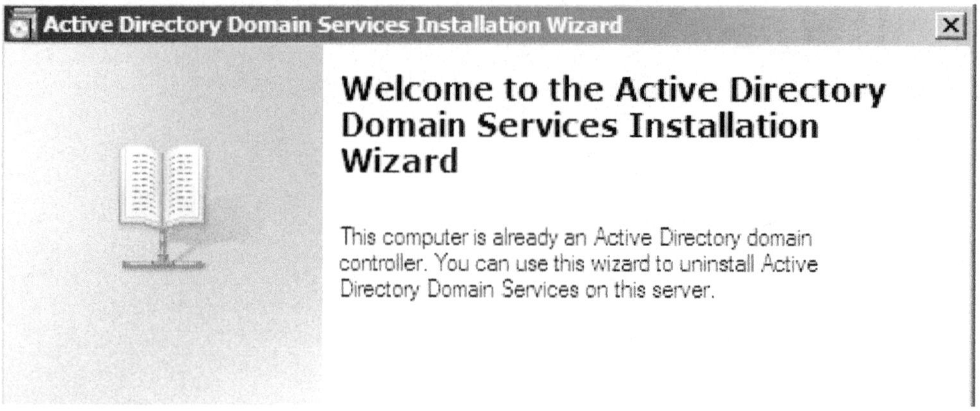

### Active Directory Domain Services Installation Wizard

**Welcome to the Active Directory Domain Services Installation Wizard**

This computer is already an Active Directory domain controller. You can use this wizard to uninstall Active Directory Domain Services on this server.

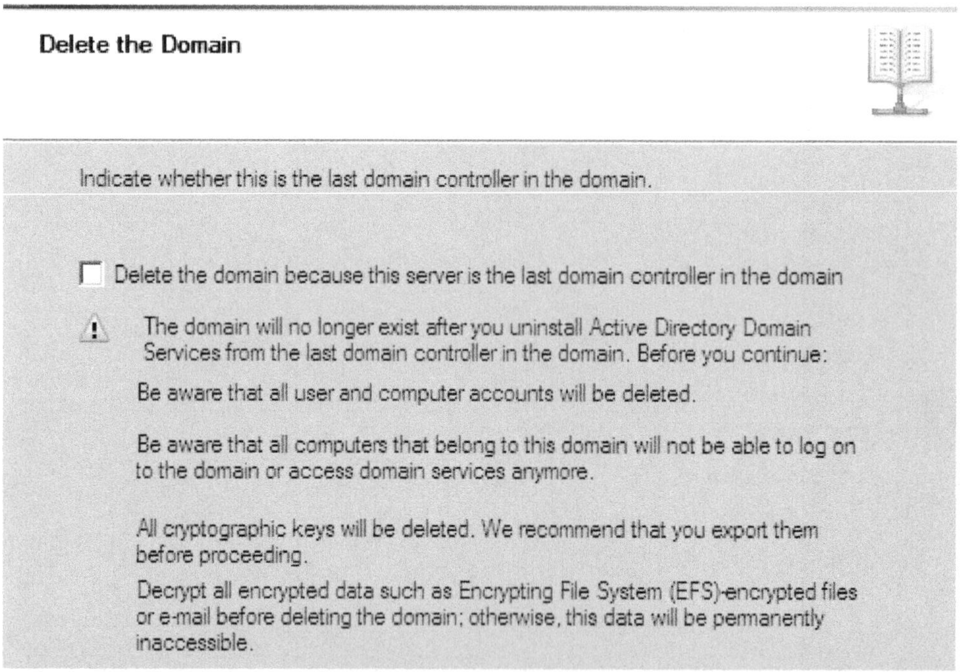

### Delete the Domain

Indicate whether this is the last domain controller in the domain.

☐ Delete the domain because this server is the last domain controller in the domain

⚠ The domain will no longer exist after you uninstall Active Directory Domain Services from the last domain controller in the domain. Before you continue:

Be aware that all user and computer accounts will be deleted.

Be aware that all computers that belong to this domain will not be able to log on to the domain or access domain services anymore.

All cryptographic keys will be deleted. We recommend that you export them before proceeding.

Decrypt all encrypted data such as Encrypting File System (EFS)-encrypted files or e-mail before deleting the domain; otherwise, this data will be permanently inaccessible.

### Active Directory Domain Services Installation Wizard

**Confirm Deletion**

Removing Active Directory Domain Services will delete all application partitions from this Active Directory domain controller.

Confirm that you want the wizard to delete all application directory partitions on this Active Directory domain controller. The partitions will be deleted when the wizard is completed.

☐ Delete all application directory partitions on this Active Directory domain controller.

⚠ Deleting the last replica of an application partition deletes all data associated with that partition.

## Roles and Operation Masters

Updating Active Directory objects can usually be performed by any domain controller unless the domain controller is read-only. After an object is updated on one, the changes will be propagated to all other domain controllers through replication. HOWEVER, some types of updates must be handled by specific Domain Controllers known as Flexible Single Master Operations FSMO roles, including

- Schema Master
- Domain Naming Master
- Infrastructure Master
- Relative ID RID Master
- Primary Domain Controller PDC Emulator

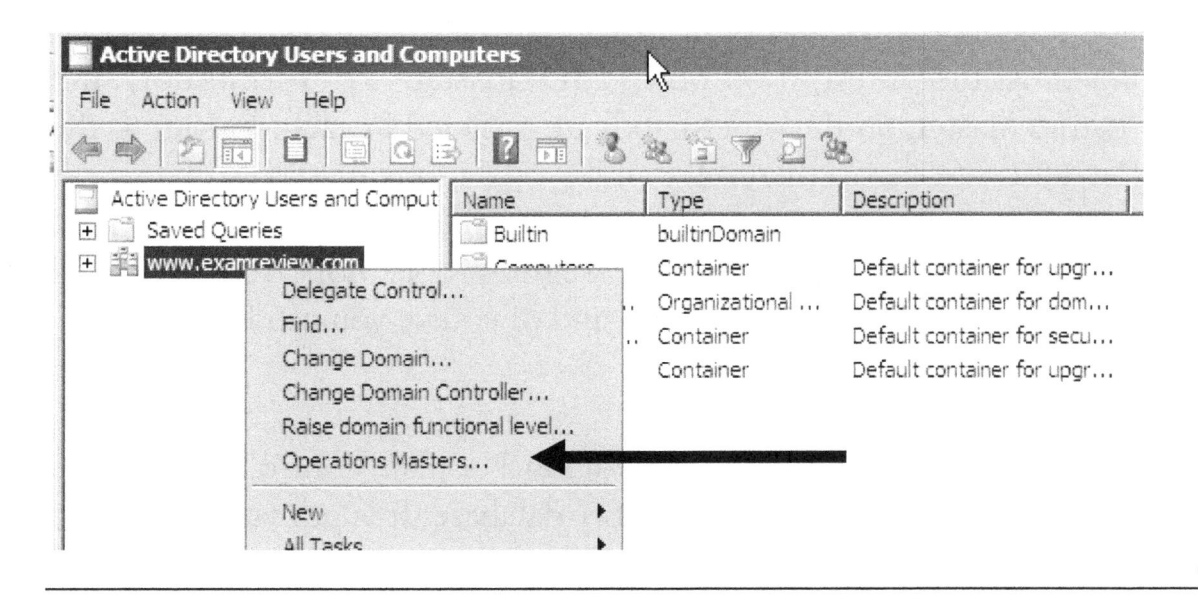

You want to know that all schema changes are processed by the Schema Master. This role is always kept in the forest root domain, and that you should place it on the same domain controller as the PDC emulator, which is the authoritative domain controller in a domain and the default domain controller for most administrative tools. In fact this PDC emulator also serves as the authoritative time source.

When domains join or leave a forest, the domain naming master makes the updates and commits the necessary changes into AD. You want this role to be performed by the PDC emulator of the forest root. Each domain needs to have its very own infrastructure master, which performs name translation between globally unique identifiers (GUIDs), security identifiers (SIDs), and distinguished names (DNs) for all foreign domain objects. Each domain also needs to have a domain controller with the RID master role to handling relative IDs arrangement. You want to have this role assigned to a domain controller that also serves as a PDC emulator.

Generally, schema master and domain naming master are assigned once in the domain at the forest root only. RID master, PCD emulator, and Infrastructure Master, on the other hand, are assigned in each domain to the same domain controller in there. A standby operations master is one which can assume the operations master role should the original computer fails. One domain controller can act as the standby operations master for all operations master roles within a domain, and of course you can have more.

A RODC Read Only DC is simply an additional domain controller that hosts read-only partitions of the Active Directory database. It is primarily for use in branch office with poor WAN link. RODC can keep cached credentials so faster login can be made possible.

You want to know that the first domain controller in a forest must NOT be an RODC. Also keep in mind, before you may install any RODC in a Windows 2000 Server or Windows Server 2003 forest, you must first prepare the forest using adprep /rodcprep. As previously said, in Windows Server 2008 R2 Adprep.exe can be found in the /support/adprep folder of the DVD disc.

**Creating new forest, new child domain or new domain tree**

When a server is already a domain controller for a domain, it cannot also act as the domain controller for another. Therefore, to create a new forest or a new domain tree or a new child domain, you need to do so on a new server. On that server you need to use Server Manager to Add Roles -> Active Directory Domain Services. Through the Active Directory Domain Services Installation Wizard you go into advanced mode installation and pick the desired options.

Although there is an add forest option in the GPMC, that is not for actually creating a new forest!

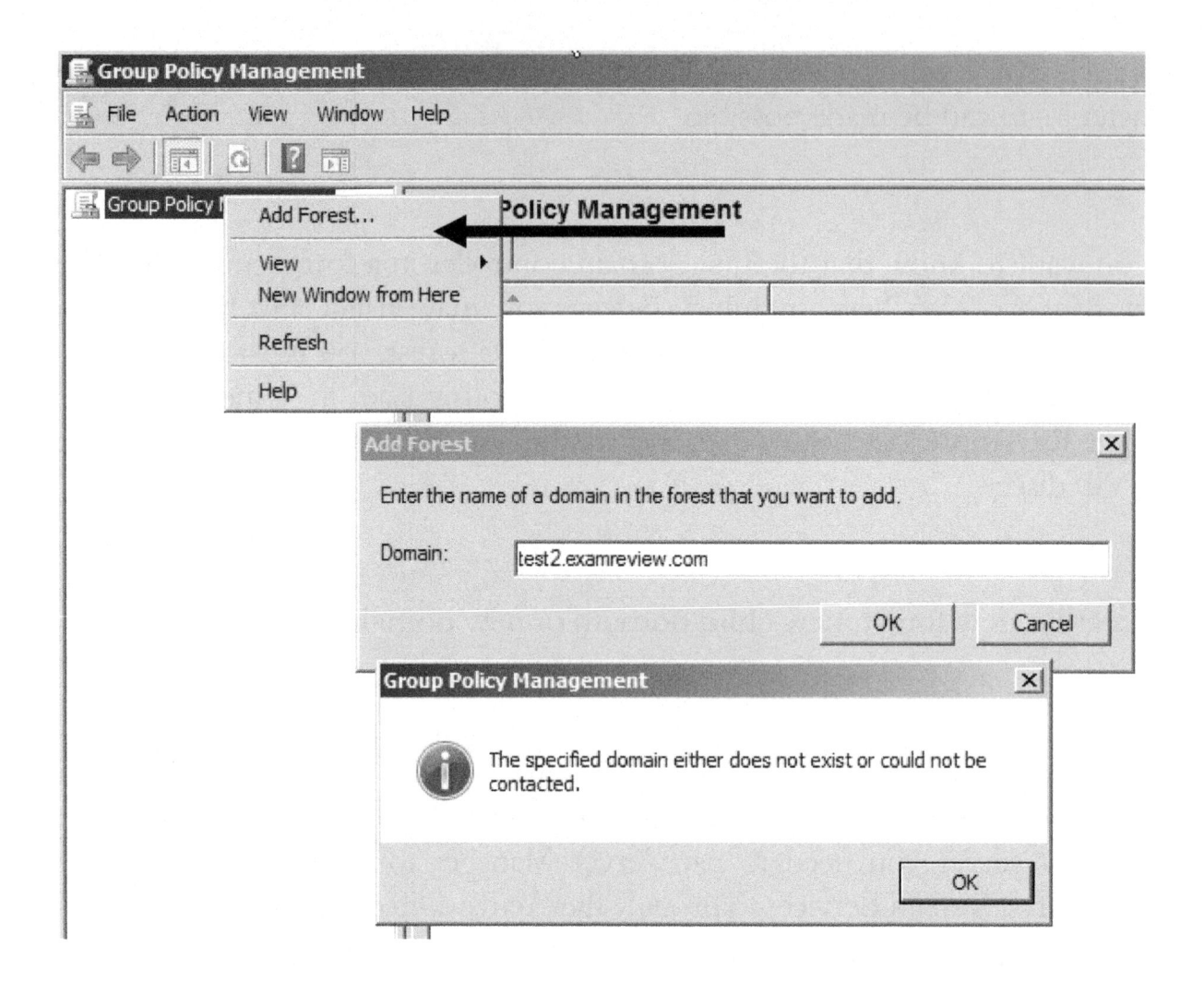

## Creating new resources, OUs and sites

You use the AD Users and Computers console to create new resources, AD users, printers, shares and OUs. On the other hand, you use the AD Sites and Services console to create and manage sites.

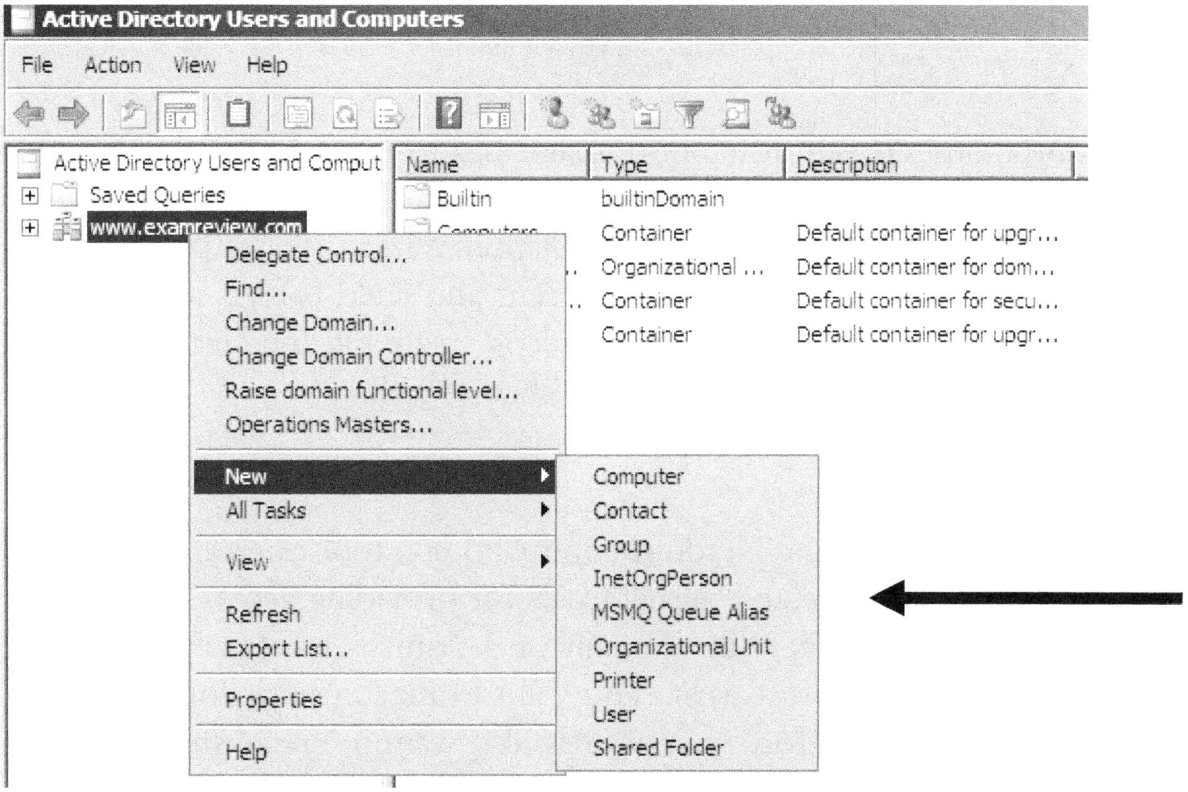
Active Directory Users and Computers
File Action View Help
Active Directory Users and Comput
Saved Queries
www.examreview.com
Name
Type
Description
Builtin
builtinDomain
Container
Default container for upgr...
Organizational ...
Default container for dom...
Container
Default container for secu...
Container
Default container for upgr...
Delegate Control...
Find...
Change Domain...
Change Domain Controller...
Raise domain functional level...
Operations Masters...
New
All Tasks
View
Refresh
Export List...
Properties
Help
Computer
Contact
Group
InetOrgPerson
MSMQ Queue Alias
Organizational Unit
Printer
User
Shared Folder

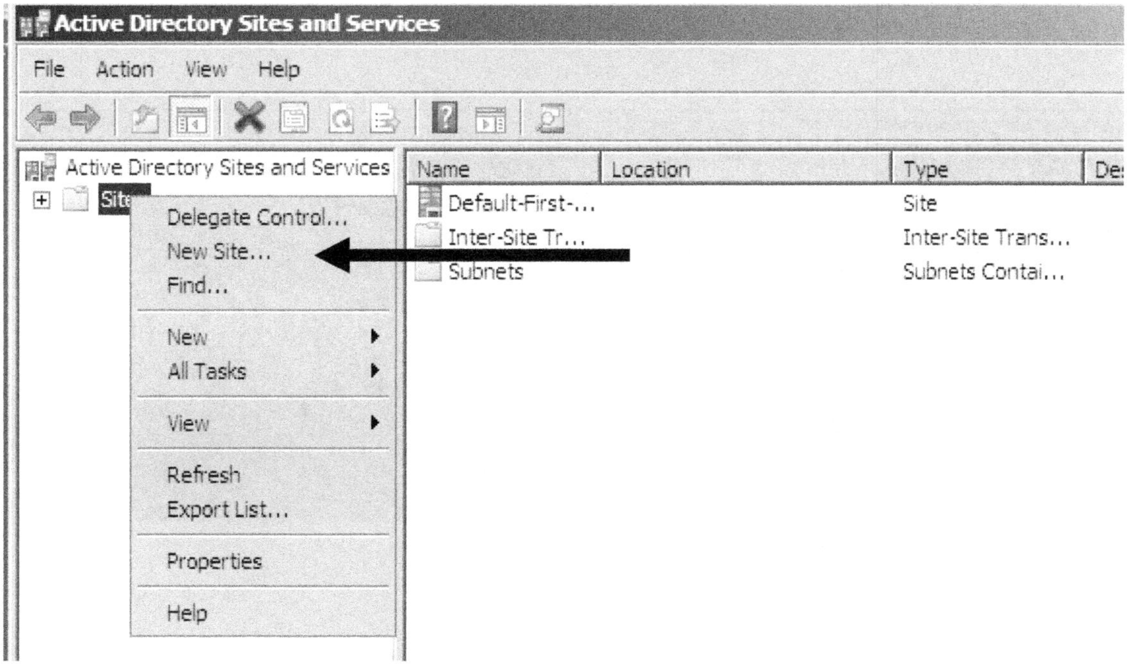
Active Directory Sites and Services
File Action View Help
Active Directory Sites and Services
Name
Location
Type
Default-First-...
Site
Inter-Site Tr...
Inter-Site Trans...
Subnets
Subnets Contai...
Delegate Control...
New Site...
Find...
New
All Tasks
View
Refresh
Export List...
Properties
Help

## Trusts

Communication between different domains has to take place through trusts, which are authentication pipelines. The necessary default trusts are created when you use the Active Directory Installation Wizard. To be precise, when a new child domain is created, a new parent and child trust is automatically established. Also, when a new domain tree is created in the current forest, a new tree-root trust is automatically established as well.

Note that you may use the Netdom command line tool to create new trusts by hand. You want to create external trusts for providing access to resources located on a Windows NT 4.0 domain or a domain located in a separate forest not joined by a forest trust. You want to make use of forest trusts to share resources between forests. You may also want to create shortcut trusts for improving user logon times between two different domains.

```
Administrator: Command Prompt
Microsoft Windows [Version 6.0.6001]
Copyright (c) 2006 Microsoft Corporation.  All rights reserved.

C:\Users\Administrator>netdom
The syntax of this command is:

NETDOM [ ADD | COMPUTERNAME | HELP | JOIN | MOVE | QUERY | REMOVE |
         MOVENT4BDC | RENAMECOMPUTER | RESET | TRUST | VERIFY | RESETPWD ]

The command completed successfully.

C:\Users\Administrator>
```

You may also use AD Domains and Trusts to call up the New Trust Wizard and achieve the same.

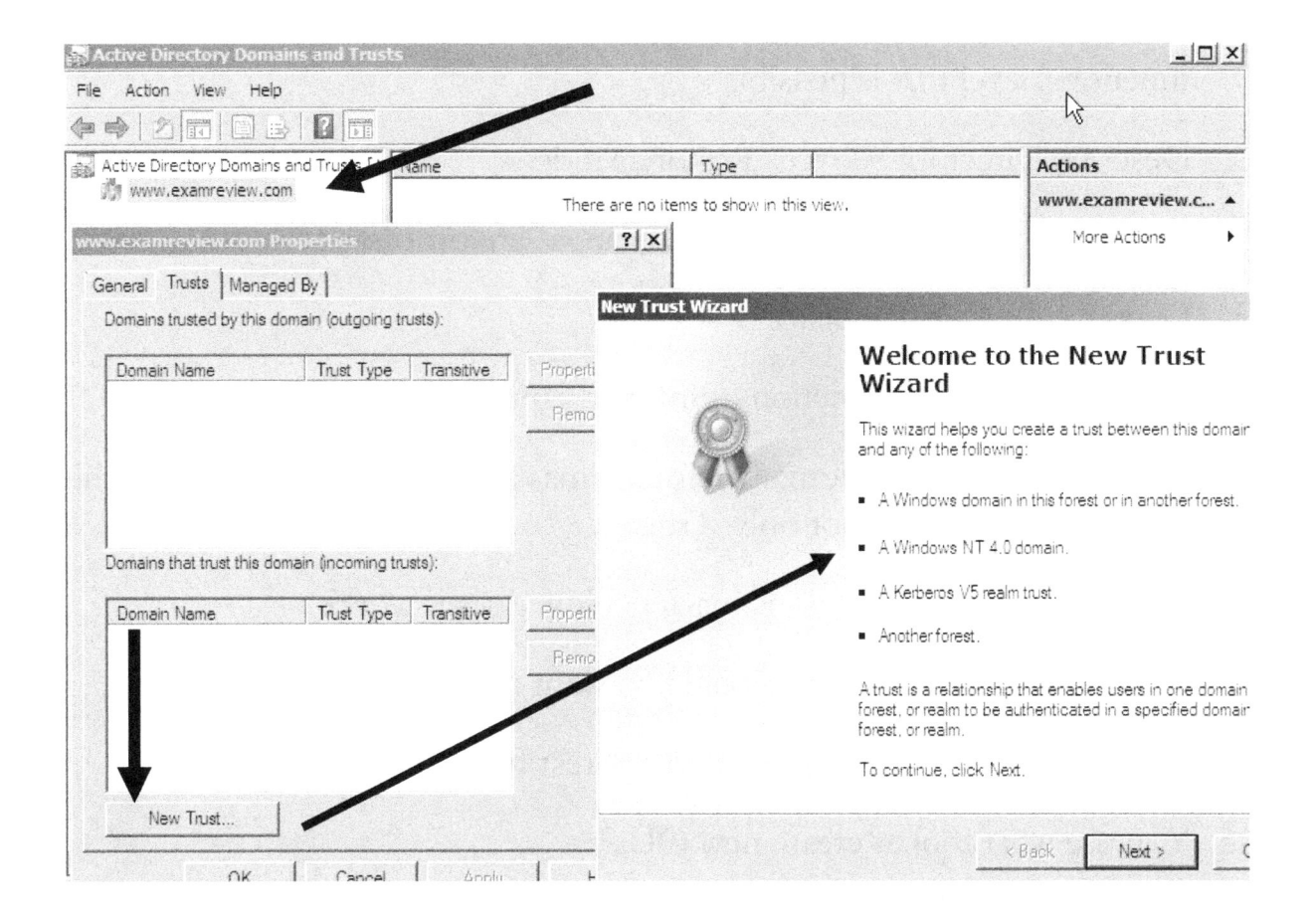

## Questions:

1. What command can you use to invoke the AD Installation Wizard?

2. How do you run the AD Installation Wizard in advanced mode?

3. AD database files include:

4. You may prepare a forest by extending the schema via what tool?

5. In Windows Server 2008 R2, Adprep.exe can be found in which location?

6. When the first Windows Server 2008–based Domain Controller is introduced, the forest will operate by default at the _____ functional level that is possible.

7. Describe Directory Services Restore Mode.

8. You want to know that all schema changes are processed by:

9. Describe the PDC emulator.

10. What is the primary function of infrastructure master?

11. Schema master and domain naming master are assigned once in the domain at the forest root only. True?

12. What is a standby operations master? How does it work?

13. What is a RODC and why would you want one?

14. What tool do you use to prepare the forest for a RODC?

15. You use what tool to create new OUs?

16. You may use what command line tool to create new trusts by hand?

17. You want to create external trusts for what purpose?

18. You want to make use of forest trusts for what purpose?

19. Why are shortcut trusts preferable?

## Answers:

1. *You need to use the dcpromo command to invoke the AD Installation Wizard.*

2. *If you use the /adv switch you can run the wizard in advanced mode.*

172

3. You need to have an NTFS partition with enough free space to hold the AD database files including the Active Directory database, the log files, and the SYSVOL shared folder. These are considered as System State data.

4. If you install a new Server 2008 R2 domain controller in an existing 2000 Server or Server 2003 based domain, and if this domain controller is also the first Windows Server 2008 R2 domain controller in the forest, you must prepare the forest by extending the schema via adprep.

5. In Windows Server 2008 R2, Adprep.exe can be found in the /support/adprep folder of the DVD disc.

6. When the first Windows Server 2008–based Domain Controller is introduced, the forest will operate by default at the lowest functional level that is possible, which is Windows 2000.

7. Directory Services Restore Mode DSRM is an alternate boot environment. With it your Windows Server can boot with the Active Directory database offline so you may perform routine maintenance as needed.

8. You want to know that all schema changes are processed by the Schema Master.

9. The PDC emulator is the authoritative domain controller in a domain and the default domain controller for most administrative tools. In fact this PDC emulator also serves as the authoritative time source.

10. Each domain needs to have its very own infrastructure master, which performs name translation between globally unique identifiers (GUIDs), security identifiers (SIDs), and distinguished names (DNs) for all foreign domain objects.

11. Generally, schema master and domain naming master are assigned once in the domain at the forest root only.

12. A standby operations master is one which can assume the operations master role should the original computer fails. One domain controller can act as the standby operations

master for all operations master roles within a domain, and of course you can have more.

13. A RODC Read Only DC is simply an additional domain controller that hosts read-only partitions of the Active Directory database. It is primarily for use in branch office with poor WAN link. RODC can keep cached credentials so faster login can be made possible.

14. Before you may install any RODC in a Windows 2000 Server or Windows Server 2003 forest, you must first prepare the forest using adprep / rodcprep.

15. You use the AD Users and Computers console to create new resources, AD users, printers, shares and OUs.

16. You may use the Netdom command line tool to create new trusts by hand.

17. You want to create external trusts for providing access to resources located on a Windows NT 4.0 domain or a domain located in a separate forest not joined by a forest trust.

18. You want to make use of forest trusts to share resources between forests.

19. You may want to create shortcut trusts for improving user logon times between two different domains.

# End of book

Made in the USA
Middletown, DE
22 October 2018